For the Term of my Legal Life

🐢 Turtle Publishing

Copyright © 2025 John Baulch QC

John Baulch has asserted his right under the Copyright, Designs and Patents Act 1988 to be identified as the author of this work. The information in this book is based on the author's experiences and opinions. The publisher specifically disclaims responsibility for any adverse consequences, which may result from use of the information contained herein.

All rights reserved. No part of this publication may be reproduced, stored in or introduced into a retrieval system, or transmitted in any form, or by any means (electronic, mechanical, photocopying, recording or otherwise) without the prior written permission of the author. Any person who does any unauthorised acts in relation to this publication will be liable to criminal prosecution and civil claims for damages. Enquiries should be made through the publisher.

First published by Turtle Publishing 2025

ISBN: 978-1-7638884-0-1 (paperback)
ISBN: 978-1-7638884-1-8 (ebook)

turtlepublishing.com.au

It's my life and I'll do what I want,

It's my mind and I'll think what I want.

From 'It's my Life' by The Animals.[1]

---

1 These works are from one of my favourite songs from my university days. As time went on and I read more of Israel Folau and Professor Ridd, they have become dearer to my heart.

Top row – Geneva, Chace, Justine, Chelsea,
Middle – Liberty, Christine, Olivia
Front – Eloise & Estella

*This book is for my wife,
Christine Margaret,*

*my daughters,
Justine Louise, Olivia Jane
and Chace Margaret*

*as well as my grandchildren
Liberty Chace, Chelsea
Iris, Geneva Portia, Estella
Christine and Eloise Cate.*

*Without their support and love
many of the events recorded
would not have occurred,
much less been written about.*

TABLE OF CONTENTS

COMMEMORATIVE TO MY HUSBAND — xi
INTRODUCTION — xiii

PART 1

Tasmania — 1
Family and Home Life — 1

PART 2

University of Tasmania, Hobart — 9

PART 3

Papua New Guinea — 17
My First Murder Trial — 21
Rabaul — 25
The Emanuel Trial – Rabaul — 40

Return to Port Moresby – May 1972 — 51
The Queen v Peter Ivara and Kasimilo Guraea — 51
The Queen v Katia, Abauwa, Kapero and Pelia — 55
The French Girls — 57
Christine — 61

Other Pacific Islands — 65
The Solomon Islands — 65
Trip to Kiribati — 66

PART 4

Townsville, Queensland   73
    The Judges in Townsville   78
    Some funny stories   79

PART 5

A Brief Return to Tasmania   81

PART 6

Return to Townsville   87
    Some Interesting Queensland Cases   87
    The Fun We Had   94

PART 7

Things that Mattered   107
    The Queen v Brian Marlin   107
    Harris and Northern Sandblasting, 1995
    QCA 413; 1997 188 CLR 313   119
    Valleyfied Pty Ltd v Primac Ltd And Anor   121
    The Queen and Smith   123
    Fingleton and the Queen   125
    Cardinal George Pell   126

PART 8

A Properly Funded Legal Aid System	165
A United, Collegiate Profession – Do We Have a Lot to Learn From the Americans?	166
Time Costing and Budgets	166
Judicial Officers Returning to the Fray	167
Accurate Reporting of Court Proceedings	169
The Business of University Education	172
The Curse of Advertising	178
The Cheating Culture	178

PART 9

Body Corporate Living	179
The Joy of Taking Offence and Political Correctness	*182*

PART 10

Regrets, I've had a Few	189
Acting for Friends and Family	*189*

ABOUT THE AUTHOR	195
FORMALITIES	197
Swearing In	*197*
Valedictory	*209*
POST SCRIPT	235

Painting of John by Kim McCubben

COMMEMORATIVE TO MY HUSBAND

John passed away on 22 November 2021, suddenly and unexpectedly.

He had been unwell with prostate cancer but in February of 2021, he broke his shoulder, which made him rather incapacitated and generally suffering a lot of pain.

He did not do very much in those last 10 months to complete his book.

He had done quite a lot towards the book after his retirement from the District Court Bench in 2017. The title is his own and a number of the earlier chapters have been completed by him.

He was extremely interested in Cardinal Pell's various Court cases and researched it all, however, did not polish it before he died.

To the best of my knowledge and of others who have helped me along the way, the remainder of the book is similar to what he would have written. If I've referenced incorrectly, it's my fault and not the fault of John or others.

I would like to particularly thank Wendy Pack KC who, early on in the piece, said to me, 'Christine, there is definitely a book in this but it is whether you are prepared to put the work into it.'

I believe I owe this to John.

I thank my daughter, Chace, whose patience and perseverance I am eternally grateful for. To Wendy Pack KC for her corrections and advice and Andrew Lowrey for his research.

Christine Baulch
Townsville
2 November 2024

INTRODUCTION

Those who know me will not be surprised to hear that I am not intending to record a lot of deep and meaningful legal thoughts in this memoir.

I have enjoyed a fulfilling and satisfying life as a lawyer and I have it in mind to share some notable moments, some of the fun and some of the thoughts of a working lawyer.

Those seeking learned legal thoughts should look elsewhere. There are plenty of Judges and lawyers who write profoundly serious books both during their judicial service and when it is finished. Some of them seem, in my opinion, to become more and more impressed with their own importance as time goes by, which can result in the books being heavy-going.

Practising law in Papua New Guinea, the Pacific Islands and Queensland had many challenges but was also great fun. Many in the profession think it would be a terrible thing if it ever got out that we had fun while practising law. I do not share that view.

All work and no play does, indeed, make Jack a dull boy.

I have had my share of bad times.

And I have had my share of good times.

The important thing is that looking back,

I would not have missed it for quids.

I hope that I will be remembered as someone who spent more time talking to people rather than about them. Those who have annoyed me most are those with such limited communication skills that they cannot wait for the end of the question before commencing to tell the questioner the answer.

PART 1
Tasmania

Family and Home Life

My parents (born 1917 and 1918 respectively) grew up towards the end of World War I, through the depression years, as well as World War II. I think the hardship of those years was something that they remembered all their lives.

Both were university graduates and placed great value on university education. My father completed a science degree in 1941 and my mother an arts degree in 1945 (both at the University of Tasmania).

My father worked as a teacher for a large part of his working life before becoming the Secretary to the Schools Board of Tasmania, a body that at first administered schools board examinations (intermediate examinations) and later matriculation (university entrance) examinations.

For the Term of my Legal Life

1954 Hobart Technical School

1954 Hobart Technical School

Dad spent 1962 as headmaster at the newly established Kings Meadows High School in Launceston. It was his second appointment as Principal. He had been the Principal of the Devonport Technical College the previous year.

I think he realised that he had gone about as far as he could with the Education Department and so took up the position of Secretary to the Schools Board of Tasmania the following year. We moved to Hobart and I undertook matriculation at the Hobart Matriculation College.

My mother taught languages, english and art at different times. But she did not work continuously, preferring, as was the way of things in those days, to have periods when she was engaged as a full-time homemaker.

I grew up in a home where hard work and application to study were part of the routine. I remember my father coming home after a day's teaching, an hour or so coaching the cricket team or the football team (depending on the time of year) and then spending an hour or so attending to his vegetable garden, before coming inside for dinner.

On weeknights, dinner and washing-up completed (as a family activity and without the assistance of an electric dishwashing machine), the whole family would often be seated at the dining table, my parents marking assignments or setting examination papers and my brother, my sister and I attending to our homework.

My parents were extremely cautious about distractions and when television first came to Tasmania (when the family was living in Launceston and I was attending Queechy High School), my father hired a television set for the duration of the school holidays, but it was always returned at the end of the relevant school holiday. My father would not contemplate having one in the house full-time. Those who subscribe to the modern view that children require constant stimulation would not be comfortable in such an environment, but I look back on those times as happy and contented times and more importantly, as times when there was time to sit and think and absorb what I was being taught and what was going on around me.

In about 1957, when we were living at Canning Street in Launceston, my father bought his first car, an FJ Holden. It was an exciting time for the whole family. My father had taken driving lessons prior to purchasing it as he had never had a car before (he was then almost 40 years old). How the world has changed. But we loved that car and very much enjoyed outings in it for picnics and the like. It was only somewhat later that I thought about how modest my father's ambitions were.

We read books and a dictionary was always readily available. My father took us on outings to the public library every fortnight or so and we returned with three or four books, which he expected we would read before the next visit to the library. We usually did and I am sure that the practice stood us in good stead for later life.

I worked hard at the Queechy High School (where I was dux of the school in my final year). I worked harder at the Hobart Matriculation College in the following year. I was not a notable student there but managed to complete my matriculation qualification in one year (where two were allowed) and accordingly enrolled at university in 1964, just before my 17th birthday.

1962 Queechy High School Rugby Union Team

1960

For the Term of my Legal Life

1962

1963

PART 2
University of Tasmania, Hobart
– Post Papua New Guinea

One of the things that I find difficult to explain to this day is why I chose to enrol in a law degree. I know I had some immature thoughts about pursuing an area of study in which my parents and my siblings would not be competitive with me but even looking back on it, they seem inadequate.

In those days it was unusual for persons from state schools to enrol in Law at the University of Tasmania. The more usual thing was to find the sons and daughters of legal practitioners or other private school students to make up each year's intake into the Law faculty. PV Manser and I were the only state school products in a class of 22 in 1964. Peter and I shared interesting times together and remain friends to this day. Over the years we became friendly with all the students of our year.

The class of '64 50 years on

What I do remember about university is the great reduction in the number of contact hours with teachers – it seemed to be the greatest freedom one could imagine. There was a library where one could catch up on things not properly understood at lectures and a large cafeteria where many hours could be spent drinking coffee, playing cards, exchanging thoughts and forming opinions. It was a great time.

I was not one of those students who wished to engage in student politics. I just revelled in the freedom of university life. I found an abundance of time for training for rugby union (an activity which I was an enthusiastic participant not burdened with talent) and for the social activity that accompanied that sport. It was a new world for me.

The Law course in those days consisted of two years of full-time university study and then three years serving what was called Articles of Clerkship (one was articled to a legal practitioner and worked in his office during ordinary office hours). The academic workload was reduced from four subjects a year to three subjects a year whilst articles were undertaken and the subjects in those latter years were generally taught in the evening at the Law Society Library in Hobart, often by members of the Tasmanian profession.

In Tasmania just before that time, students had paid the practitioner for the privilege of serving Articles of Clerkship. That finished not all that long before I started my articles. I was paid about $11 a week in my first year of articles and $15 a week in my second year of articles. Had it been necessary for me to serve the third year I think I would have been paid something of the order of $20 a week. Fortunately, I avoided that by securing employment as Associate to Mr Justice Chambers for that third year and found myself a recipient of wages in excess of $100 a week. I had never dreamt of having so much money.

As to articles, I learned how to file documents in the Court of Requests (the civil jurisdiction of Magistrates at the time), the Supreme Court, the Companies Registry, the Land Titles Registry and little else. I do know that performing these activities on behalf of firms that operated from Melbourne and Sydney was a great part of my work and that my employers did well from the fees that I generated as an articled law clerk.

I was very much amused when my good friend Robert Douglas Pack ('RD'), who will be mentioned more than once as I proceed, referred to an Articled Law Clerk as 'the lowest form of legal life'. That is certainly how it felt to me.

When I was preparing to write this memoir, I was surprised to find that Mr Max Bull, of Messrs Lewis Driscoll and Bull (the solicitor to whom I was articled to in 1966 and 1967), had provided me with a reference in which he spoke rather highly of me.

In 1968, I acquired the job of Associate to the then newly appointed Mr Justice Chambers of the Tasmanian Supreme Court. I learned more in that year than I had learned in the four years of legal study prior to my appointment as his Associate.

Mr Justice Chambers was a very conservative man. He would not attend social functions involving lawyers without having me in attendance and he made it clear to me that the purpose of my being there was to ensure that he was not inappropriately approached or spoken to by anyone present. When we travelled away on circuit in Tasmania (to Launceston and Burnie), he preferred that I have dinner with him in the restaurant at the hotels we stayed at so that he would never be alone in public. If for any reason I was not available, he preferred room service to dining alone in the dining room.

He was much admired by the profession and I count myself lucky to have spent that year with him. He was always courteous and considerate in the Courtroom, saving any demonstration of his irritation about the behaviour of counsel and litigants until he had retired to his chambers. I often thought about him when I was serving as a Judge of the District Court of Queensland because I think it is a measure of one's self-control if one can always do that. I tried to follow his example, but I fear that I did not always succeed.

My first year after admission was spent in Burnie in North West Tasmania. Being a young man without connections in the legal profession in Tasmania at the time did not, as I have already said, auger well for one's chances of success in the profession.

I eventually managed to secure employment at the office of Messrs BS Sproule and McLean (in Burnie) at a salary of about 70% of what I had been paid as the Judge's Associate. Within a short time, I was bored stiff.

The people I acted for in that time were what were then referred to as 'deserted wives' and the struggle to obtain and/or enforce maintenance orders in the Magistrates Court was played out in an arena that was quite one-sided in favour of the deserting husband and successful days were few and far between.

The partners who employed me were Mr Basil Sproule and Mr Geoff McLean, the latter being a recent graduate of the University of Tasmania. The partners were less than helpful to a new graduate and I spent many hours in my little office watching the clock go around waiting until it was time to go to rugby union training.

I was so frustrated with that employment that I responded to an advertisement that I saw in a national magazine (*The Bulletin* – published in Sydney), seeking expressions of interest from lawyers wishing to work in Papua New Guinea.

Within a few days, I received a telephone call from a man in Sydney who advised of his intention to fly to Tasmania to interview me about a position. Shortly after that phone call he arrived in Burnie and spoke with me about the position and a few days later I was offered a position in the Department of Law in Port Moresby.

No specific job was offered (just employment in the Department of Law) but I was told that my starting salary would be a little more than $10,000 per annum (almost three times what I was receiving in Burnie) and that the tax rate would be significantly less than the Australian tax rate. It did not take me long to decide and I arranged that I would start in Port Moresby early in the new year.

Thinking that I should do the right thing by my then employers, I advised them that I would not return to Burnie in the new year but that I would stay on until Christmas time while they thought about replacing me. They thanked me for showing that consideration, but their gratitude was short-lived. A few days later, they advised me that they had given some thought to the matter and that they had decided that the best course was to terminate my employment immediately.

I was a little taken aback at the time, but it was a good life lesson.

Looking back on it, I am pleased that things worked out that way as it gave me time to spend with my parents in Hobart, which I would not otherwise have had as it was not then certain what I should do with the rest of my life but there was at least a possibility, which later became a reality, that I would only return to Tasmania from time to time on holidays once I departed for Papua New Guinea.

I spent a very pleasant few months in Hobart with my parents before going to Papua New Guinea, and am very pleased that I did, as by the time I returned to Hobart in 1975, my mother was not well and my father was finding it extremely difficult to look after her. My absence in PNG meant that I missed some contact with my mother before she became unwell and I am sad about that because, before illness overtook her, she was a very interesting and talented person.

I have managed to maintain contact with Tasmania and with my Tasmanian friends to this day and we often reminisce about the happy times we had during our university days. Some of the happiest recollections of Tasmania revolve around my father and my university friends.

While my father was a conservative and sometimes difficult man, he always had the best interests of his children at heart. More than once he assisted me with unusual expenses that arose from my unrestrained behaviour while a student.

His very strict approach to things has always been with me:

> '... but he was more than just a father,
>
> a teacher, my best friend,
>
> though he may be gone,
>
> memories linger on,
>
> and I miss him,
>
> the old man.'

Taken from 'The Old Man', a favourite Irish song of mine

PART 3
Papua New Guinea

I do not think I will ever forget arriving in Port Moresby. Having been brought up in Tasmania and never having travelled further north than Melbourne and Sydney, I was completely unprepared for the heat.

On arrival at Jacksons Airport in Port Moresby in early January 1970, I began to move forward in the aircraft to disembark. I was puzzled by the somewhat casual behaviour of the rest of the passengers as it seemed to me that something must be on fire, but it was just the heat radiating from the tarmac outside the aircraft.

I was met and transported to a hostel that provided comfortable, but not luxurious accommodation for public servants in the Territory. Meals (of reasonable quality) were served in a nearby cafeteria. The rooms were not self-contained but the shared bathroom facilities were quite adequate.

I was told that I should present myself at the Public Solicitor's Office on the following morning. Those matters having been attended to, my guide departed.

I had met a man from Western Australia on the aircraft who, like me, was new to the Territory and had been delivered to the same hostel. When our guide departed the hostel, we decided it would be a good idea to do a little exploration by ourselves and we called a taxi and asked to be taken to a hotel. We were delivered to the Boroko Hotel a little distance away from the hostel.

We went into a beer garden. It seemed to me to be a curious place because the first thing I noticed was that all the furniture was set into the concrete floor so that it was not movable or adjustable in any way at all. The second thing of note was that when one went to the bar one could see that there were metal grids which had been pulled up towards the ceiling but could be quickly released and would slot into holes in the bar service area leaving the bar quite secure from the public area. I was later to learn that these grids were commonplace in hotels and served to protect bar staff from hostile patrons at closing time.

My companion and I purchased beers and sat down to soak up the atmosphere. There were quite a few people in the beer garden, but it could not be said that it was crowded.

After a while, a man in a military uniform with a large, polished brass 'E' on his shirt approached us. I had yet to learn the significance of the 'E' on the shirt of military personnel in Papua New Guinea. It meant that the wearer was proficient in the English language. This, I came to understand, was particularly useful information in Papua New Guinea.

This man explained to me and my companion that we were taking a significant risk by drinking in the beer garden. He said that this area was generally only for the native population. A quick inspection of the customers revealed that my companion and I were indeed the only expatriates in the beer garden. Our new acquaintance told us that we could find a more suitable bar area inside the hotel. He also told us that there were people in the beer garden discussing how much money we might be expected to be in possession of and how they could most efficiently remove it from us.

He said that if we did not wish to go into the European part of the hotel, we would be welcome to come with him to the sergeant's mess at the military barracks.

This seemed to us to be a really good idea and we accompanied him and three or four of his friends to the sergeant's mess where we had a very enjoyable time over two or three hours before he arranged for us to be transported back to the hostel.

Looking back on that evening, I think that my guardian angel was watching over me because things would have gone seriously wrong but for our good fortune to encounter that man.

The next morning, I reported to the Public Solicitor's Office as instructed. That office was in the heart of Port Moresby.

The first person I met was Peter Lalor, the then Public Solicitor. He was dressed in sports trousers, a short-sleeved white shirt undone almost to the navel and white shoes with no laces. Little did I know then that he was to become one of the most significant influences in my legal life.

He took me on a tour of the office and introduced me to other staff who worked there before leaving me in a back room with a few files to read 'just to get an idea of what things were like in the Territory'. (He always referred to Papua New Guinea as the Territory).

After a couple of hours reading these files, the receptionist came to me and said that there was a man at the front counter who wanted to speak to me. I told her that I thought she must have made a mistake as I had only arrived in the Territory the previous day and as far as I was aware, I didn't know anybody at all in Port Moresby. She said she was quite sure that there was no mistake because this man even knew how to spell my name (I suppose in Papua New Guinea that was always a bit of a test).

I went with her to the front counter and there I met Tony Fraser who told me that he had come to see me because he had been told that I was a rugby union player and he wished to make sure that I did not bind myself to any other club than the one that he belonged to.

We had coffee together that morning and by the time he departed, it had been agreed that I would go to training with the Colleagues Fari Rugby Union Club. Before the end of the week, I attended a couple of training sessions, but nothing much ever came of it as I was posted to Rabaul. There I played a season and a half with the Nonga Hospital Rugby Union team before deciding that PNG was no place to play rugby union unless one was particularly dedicated to fitness (which I was not). My association with that hospital rugby union team is a story for another time.

After a few days, a friend from my university days in Tasmania, Kerry Dillon, arrived in Port Moresby from Rabaul where he had been working. He introduced me to Clive Wall (later Wall QC in Townsville and later still a Judge of the District Court in Townsville and on the Gold Coast) and I spent a couple of days and evenings with these two men getting a picture of what it was like to live and work in PNG.

On one of the evenings we spent together, we were travelling about in Clive's Volkswagen when we were involved in a motor vehicle accident. Clive was driving, but the accident was in no way his fault. Somehow, he and Kerry Dillon both ended up with broken noses while I was uninjured.

We were all somewhat inebriated and when taken to the hospital, I was a little surprised to be asked by the doctors on duty to advise them as to the setting of my friends' noses. I think Clive always felt that I got his wrong. I did not really know them well enough prior to the hospital visit to comment but I used to assure him that I had done my best.

My First Murder Trial
in Menyamya in the Morobe Province of the Highlands

When I had been in PNG for only a couple of weeks Peter Lalor suggested to me that I should conduct the defence in a murder trial in Menyamya. This seemed to me a rather daunting prospect and I think that Peter could tell that. He assured me that the trial would be presided over by Mr Justice Frost who was a very nice person and would make sure that I did not get myself into any trouble.

I spent several sleepless nights poring over the trial materials. What might have seemed to a more experienced practitioner a straightforward self-defence case was, to me, a terrifying prospect.

The accused had been in a fight with the deceased. He had been found by the Kiap (an administration officer/policeman) with significant injuries including the amputation of one arm. The deceased had incredibly significant head and other injuries and had passed away prior to the arrival of the Kiap. Two stone axes were located at the scene.

The accused was barely conscious when the Kiap arrived but he was able to tell the Kiap that he had killed the deceased. The Kiap then loaded him into the back of their vehicle (along with the deceased) and the two stone axes and transported them to the morgue and the hospital about four hours away.

The accused surprisingly, at least from my point of view, made a quick recovery and was able to be formally interviewed by the Kiap within a day or two. He recounted the fight to the Kiap. It had been instigated by the deceased and he gave significant detail about the way in which he had gained the upper hand. He told the Kiap that he had killed the accused and that he had meant to do that. He offered no further explanation (significant admissions where the charge was to be one of wilful murder).

The Kiap then arranged for his Court appearance and a committal proceeding followed. At the conclusion of the committal proceeding the Magistrate announced that he was satisfied that there was sufficient evidence to commit the accused for trial on a charge of wilful murder. Asked whether he had anything to say in response to the charge, the accused volunteered that it was true that he had killed the man and that he had meant to do so. He was remanded in custody to the sittings of the Court at which I was to appear for him.

When I met him, he was able to confirm all those details (through the interpreter) but when I tried to discuss the concept of self-defence with him, he seemed to have little understanding of it and indeed, little interest in it.

The law in Papua New Guinea at the time permitted Counsel to enter a plea of not guilty on behalf of the accused regardless of what he said when asked to answer the indictment.

It was necessary for me to do that as when arraigned, the accused, speaking through the Court supplied interpreters, helpfully informed Justice Frost that he had indeed killed the man and that he had meant to do so.

Notwithstanding the accused's unhelpful contribution to the discussion, I did not have much trouble persuading Mr Justice Frost to enter a plea of not guilty on the basis that there was an arguable defence.

The trial took place in a large grass hut with open sides. The local population gathered on the grass outside the building where they could see and hear what was happening. I became aware during the course of the trial that there was a bit to be learned from the crowd because they knew a fair bit about what had happened and what the allegations were and were given to making sharp intakes of breath if they thought that anybody was telling less than the truth, the whole truth and nothing but the truth.

This experience was to stand me in good stead for later trials in the Territory.

After the trial had been proceeding for a short time, Mr Justice Frost advised me that he could not see the accused. To me, this was a quite unexpected and somewhat startling development. The trial Judge invited me to look at the dock and see whether the accused was present. I did so and he was indeed present, but he was lying on the floor apparently asleep. The police officer assigned to guard him woke him up and I made a pretty poor attempt to convey to him that it was important that he stay awake and listen to the evidence.

The Judge was less than satisfied with my explanation and embarked on a long explanation through the interpreters. He informed the accused that he was charged with wilful murder and that the possible penalty for wilful murder was death by hanging, and that he should pay attention to the proceedings so that he could assist his lawyer in the event that anything that was said was incorrect. He then asked the accused if he understood.

For the Term of my Legal Life

This prompted a long exchange between the accused and the interpreters. Finally, the interpreter interpreting into English told the Judge that what the accused had said was that it was true that he killed the deceased and that he meant to do it and that he had told the Magistrate that he had killed the deceased and meant to do it. He went on to say that when he came to this 'big' Court he had told the 'big' Judge that he had killed the deceased and that he had meant to do it.

He said that he was aware the Lawyer (me) had told the Judge that he did not kill the deceased and that it seemed to him that the 'big' Judge agreed with the lawyer. So he concluded it was a matter for the Lawyer and the Judge, not him.

I was learning a bit about Papua New Guinea on the run.

The trial proceeded to what I think now was its inevitable conclusion – that the accused was not guilty by reason of the fact that he had acted in self-defence. When informed of this, the accused launched into another diatribe. Eventually, the Court interpreters were able to tell us that he was enquiring about what he should do now because he could not go home because if he did so, the relatives of the deceased man would kill him by way of a payback.

This posed a real problem, which was resolved eventually on the basis that the Kiap would find some work for the accused to do around the station at Menyamya until things settled down in the village.

The lesson I learned is that the concept of self-defence was probably not a subject of after-dinner conversation in the hills around Menyamya.

I am still in possession of the stone axe which the accused gave to me at the conclusion of the trial. He said it was the axe that he had used to kill a man, but I'm not sure about that. It might just have been a similar one. Whatever the case, it is a fearsome weapon.

Rabaul

It was shortly after I returned to Port Moresby from what I can now describe, with the wisdom of hindsight, as a forensic victory, that I was asked to go to Rabaul and operate the Public Solicitor's Office over there. The area involved included New Britain and New Ireland.

Again, I was a little nervous about the prospect of running an office on the island on my own. Lalor, however, was most reassuring. He told me that if I encountered any difficulty at all I should just ring him, and he would be able to provide assistance or advice.

Lalor drove me to the airport with my suitcase of belongings. On the way, he told me that he had bought me a present to take to Rabaul with me. He gave it to me on the way, inviting me to look at it straightaway.

In a brown paper bag, I found another brown paper bag and a roll of sticky tape. I was a little puzzled until Lalor explained to me that the idea was that I should stick the paper bag on the wall in my accommodation or in the office, the only requirement being that the wall should be white. His advice then was that I should touch the paper bag on my way in or out of the room on entering and leaving. He told me that if it ever got to the stage that I couldn't see the paper bag, I should ring him straight away, and he would arrange for me to return to Port Moresby to be more closely supervised.

It was exceptionally good advice although delivered in a rather unusual way for, as I was to find over the years that followed, the Tolai people, while very nice, gentle people, did not look kindly on expatriates who associated with their women.

Notwithstanding offers and invitations given to me during the time I was in Rabaul, I stuck with Lalor's advice and did not fraternise with the Tolai population other than as was necessary for work and very limited social purposes. I am sure that is what contributed to my good relationship with the Tolai community all the time I as in Rabaul.

I was a little disappointed about the offer of telephone assistance. After I had been in Rabaul for a week or so I decided to take Lalor up on that but when I attempted to place the call, the switchboard told me that it would be necessary to wait a week or so and to book the call in. There was certainly no prospect of making a call on the day and at the time I wished to seek the assistance. I put it down to being just another of Lalor's jokes and decided I had better just do the best I could, which is what I did.

It would be silly to say that I was made welcome in Rabaul initially.

Housing for members of the public service was controlled by an interesting person named Bruce Daff. He was known as 'Curly' Daff, I assume because he was bald. He was a long-term public servant, who I think had no intention of leaving the Territory and probably would have been unemployable in any significant role in Australia.

On our first meeting, he made it quite clear to me that he thought it was a foolish thing that the government made legal aid available to the native population and that he had no intention of trying to make life easy for anyone involved with the Public Solicitor's Office.

In my youthful enthusiasm (having conducted one murder trial for one acquittal) I told him that I didn't think that his views about the social value of the Public Solicitor's Office had anything to do with much at all and that I was quite prepared to sit it out at the Kaivuna (a

Tolai word meaning 'eating place') Motel until he came to his senses.

The Kaivuna Motel was indeed a pleasant place where, in the Territory tradition, one ordered by numbers as the wait staff did not understand any of the English words printed on the menu. For dinner, for example, one might order a number two, a number five, and a number eight and these would be delivered efficiently. Newcomers to town who tried to order by describing the dish in the English words found life exceedingly difficult.

Even so, after about six weeks, the menu was becoming a little repetitious and I must say that I was becoming somewhat concerned as to the cost that the government was shelling out for my accommodation because of Daff's intransigent approach to the provision of accommodation for me.

I told Lalor about this on the telephone and he suggested that I should come to Port Moresby for the weekend so I prepared myself to be in Port Moresby on Monday morning when we would visit the Secretary for Law together to discuss my accommodation requirements.

So off I went to Port Moresby for the weekend. I spent a very pleasant weekend at a hotel overlooking Ella Beach before meeting Lalor in the office on Monday morning. In his usual rather abrupt way, he said we were off to see the Secretary for Law (a person named Lindsay Curtis who I came to understand was intensely disliked by Lalor – it was probably a mutual feeling).

On the way I enquired what, if any, speaking part I was going to have when we met with the Secretary for Law. He said I should just follow his lead.

When we were eventually shown into Curtis's office, Lalor proceeded to explain to him that I was a bright young man from Tasmania who had only been in the Territory for a few months but was proposing to return to Tasmania because Daff wouldn't give him accommodation in Rabaul. I simply nodded when it seemed appropriate. After a short discussion, Curtis assured me and Lalor that accommodation would be available by the time I got back to Rabaul.

It was.

When I received the keys from Daff, I was conscious of several junior staff at Treasury surreptitiously looking over their half walls to observe.

Daff was grumpy and had little to say. I did not speak beyond inviting him to write the address on a piece of paper, which he did. He then made a mistake, asking if I needed to be guided to the address. I told him not to bother as I had some native contacts who would show me the way. This was too much for some of the Treasury staff, whose giggles followed me out the door.

The accommodation, as it turned out, was quite comfortable. It was part of a duplex building that had a large living area, a kitchen, one bedroom and an adequate bathroom.

Above, I have already said something about the welcome that I received in Rabaul concerning accommodation. There was a great deal to learn about racial relations as well.

Very early in my time in Rabaul, I acted on behalf of a Tolai police officer. He was a young man who had risen to the rank of Sub-Inspector of Police. He was charged with a disciplinary offence over describing his superior officer in Rabaul as a 'stupid *****'.

When I met with him, I had to explain to him that truth was not a defence and that whether or not his comment was accurate was not something that he would be wise to pursue in the disciplinary hearing.

He was a clever man and understood me straight away. He did, however, proceed to explain to me at some length that he had joined the police force as a way of trying to assist the Australian administration. He told me that he did not particularly enjoy the work because he was required to enforce the law against his fellow Tolai. He told me that he would be just as happy to remain in his village and care for his family by means of fishing and gardening (the whole of the Gazelle Peninsular was blessed with very fertile soil and an abundance of fish in the nearby waters).

It took me some time to persuade him that he should not rush into a decision, that the smarter course would be to plead guilty and make an apology and that hopefully, I would persuade the Tribunal that no other penalty would be imposed.

That is how things turned out.

Within a very short time, I was approached by a Chimbu man named Berenat Nodofu who advised me that he was an experienced hausboi (an expression quite common then in Papua New Guinea but one which seems rather unfortunate now) and that because he was working as the hausboi for my neighbour in the duplex he would be able to conveniently look after me as well. That seemed a sensible idea to me and so began a relationship that continued throughout my time in Papua New Guinea, notwithstanding some tension when Berenat had to deal with my marriage and Christine's idea that she should give some directions to him, notwithstanding his, by then, quite long-standing relationship with me.

By the time I left Papua New Guinea, he and his wife resided in servant's accommodation that was provided at the Public Solicitor's house in Rabaul with their two children, one of whom had been born during the time he worked for me and was named John.

Chimbu men were somewhat feared in Papua New Guinea. I came to understand that having Berenat living on-site meant that security was not a problem I needed to concern myself with.

I will share with you some events that occurred involving Berenat that will explain the attachment we developed to one another.

When I was posted back to Port Moresby in 1972, I was offered and accepted accommodation in a house at Tokarara (a rather new superb of Port Moresby). Berenat and his family found accommodation not far away with other Chimbu people. The house that was allocated to me had a vacant block next door. Berenat and I had often talked about growing vegetables and he enquired whether there would be any problem growing some vegetables on the vacant block. I told him I could not imagine there would be, and I would help him to plant some tomatoes and, if he wished to, he could plant whatever else he wished. He was very pleased with this arrangement.

I went and obtained some bags of blood and bone, which had been one of my father's favourite gardening additives and Berenat brought some of his wantoks (literally men who spoke the same language as he did – Chimbu men) for what amounted to a working bee. We dug up a significant area on the vacant block and dug in the blood and bone. The next week, I brought home some tomato seedlings and he and his friends arrived with some other plants of different kinds and we planted them all out on this block.

Our garden was very successful (in PNG you could practically watch things grow) but Berenat and his friends were convinced that the blood and bone had special powers and asked whether they could take the bags away so that they could show them to their friends and use it to create gardens in other parts. I was happy for them to do that and Berenat often mentioned to me after that time how impressed his friends were with my knowledge about gardening.

If they had known that having seen that, they had seen everything I knew, I cannot imagine they would have been so impressed.

We were troubled by burglars only a couple of times while we were in PNG.

A notable event occurred in Port Moresby while we were living at Tokarara. We held a party in the house on the Saturday night and when it was concluded I gave Berenat and his friends some leftover drinks to take home with them. They were very taken with this.

On Sunday night we stayed away from the house and when we returned on Monday, we found that the house had been burgled and that Berenat was not in attendance as he should have been. He arrived a little time later showing obvious signs of a very significant hangover and as soon as he saw what had happened in the house it was obvious that he felt he might have been a suspect because of his failure to attend work on time.

He assured me that he knew nothing of what had happened but that he and his friends would go to the Koki market and they would find out if there was any sign of people wearing my clothes because he thought they would stand out a bit (so did I).

He returned the next morning and reported to me that he and his friends had been successful in locating some people wearing clothes that he knew were mine and they had taken them to the police station at Boroko. He wanted to know whether he should do anything about attempting to recover the clothes for me. I told him that he should not worry. I was prepared to put the matter behind me.

However, Berenat must have felt there was unfinished business to settle because the next I heard was that I should go to the Boroko Police Station where Berenat was also in police custody. I did that and learned that the police had taken the offenders to the house in Tokarara to do a walk-through demonstration of how they got into the house and where they went to obtain the items of property that had been recovered. After they had done that, they were leaving the property with the police when Berenat appeared from underneath the house wielding a sarif (a long steel implement used in PNG for cutting the grass) and before the police could stop him he had inflicted a significant wound on one of the offenders.

I spoke briefly with Berenat and he confirmed the truth of what the police had told me and said he had no complaints about the way he had been treated by the police.

My next task was to talk to the police and see whether there was any way out of this for him. Interestingly, one of the police officers involved had previously been stationed in Rabaul and knew me quite well. We eventually were able to agree upon cash bail of 50 kina which would be forfeited if Berenat failed to appear at the Court. I was happy with that outcome so I paid the 50 kina and took Berenat home. It was only sometime later that I realised that there was no bail documentation completed and I rather think that the 50 kina never made it into any official fund.

The incident did, however, reinforce Berenat's view that I had some magic powers at the police station.

While we were living at Tokarara, I gained an insight into Berenat's regard for persons from other language groups.

We were minding a dog named Soho for some friends, Vicki and Jim Stannard, who had gone on leave. The dog was not particularly attached to any person with coloured skin and used to follow Berenat around the yard growling at him and occasionally nipping at his heels. Berenat never seemed to be upset by this and would just growl back and eventually, there was a sort of truce between them.

One afternoon, however, I returned from work to find a man in a government uniform had climbed a tree in the front of the house and Soho was sitting at the base of the tree keeping an eye on him and fairly obviously proposing to attack him if he came down. I had the following conversation with Berenat.

'Do you know that there is a man up the tree?'

'Yes.'

'When did he get up there?'

'This morning.'

'Wouldn't it be a good idea to tie the dog up so that he could come down?'

'He is from Papua.'

It seemed, at least to Berenat, that no other explanation was necessary.

Whether at work or home, every day was a learning experience in PNG.

In all the time that he worked for me, he was fiercely loyal to me and totally disinterested in the welfare of any members of any racial group but his own.

When we were living in Rabaul, Berenat was very excited when his friends who worked at the Travelodge Motel were invited to the Travelodge Motel staff Christmas party and invited him to go with them.

The next morning, when I got out of bed, Gineveppa (his wife) was sitting on the back steps waiting to speak to me. She was smiling and giggling so much it was difficult for me to understand what it was she wanted to tell me but eventually she made it clear to me that Berenat had been arrested, as she understood it, for urinating on a policeman, and was presently detained in the Rabaul watchhouse.

I said I would go to the police station and see what could be done. When I got there, I found that Gineveppa was not the only person who found the whole situation somewhat amusing. All the expatriate police as well as a good number of the national members of the police force could barely contain themselves while they told me of the events that had led to Berenat's arrest.

It appears that he had been making his way home, heavily intoxicated, when he was overtaken by an urge to urinate. He had told the police that he took shelter behind what he thought was a tree and was urinating on the tree. The tree, however, turned out to be a constable of police who must have been so bored and standing so still that Berenat, in his intoxicated condition, made this mistake.

I discussed the matter with some of the more senior police officers and we decided that it would be embarrassing for everybody if the matter went to Court and we eventually decided that the best solution would be that Berenat could be released upon me depositing cash bail and if he failed to appear at the Court the cash bail would be forfeited and nothing more would be heard of it.

I paid (five kina, I think), Berenat was produced to me and we went home together after he had filled in a document which I explained to him required him to go to Court on the following Monday morning.

When we got home, I explained to him and Gineveppa that they should not go to Court on the Monday morning but leave the bail paper with me and that nothing more should be heard about the matter.

That was how things turned out.

Berenat had always thought that I had some special influence over the police, but after this event, he and his wife were convinced that I did.

When Christine and I left New Guinea, I offered to repatriate the family to the Chimbu, and that offer was accepted. We had a rather sad parting at the airport. I wrote to him on a couple of occasions but never heard from him. I expect my letters were probably incorrectly delivered or just went astray.

I returned to Rabaul in June 1972 for the second time, this time to act as Deputy Public Solicitor. Christine came with me, as we had married in Port Moresby in May 1972.

After a short time, I was invited to join what was called a Duk-Duk. The Duk-Duk was a very important part of Tolai society, operating something like a vigilante group that conducted warning raids in the nighttime where necessary and who sometimes inflicted physical punishments on people who did not behave appropriately in the village.

My introduction to the Duk-Duk consisted of spending a night with its members on Matupit Island (a very small island just off the township of Rabaul) and then taking part in a ceremonial canoe trip and procession through the village shortly after dawn. From my point of view, it was unfortunate that an ABC film crew was in attendance at the village when we landed because I was sure that somehow my parents would see this and be concerned for me. If they did see it, they never mentioned it to me, and I didn't think it was necessary to raise the topic with them because I'm quite sure that my mother, if not my father as well, would have been of the view that I must've taken leave of my senses to be involved in such a thing.

Much later, when Christine and I were living in the house provided for the Deputy Public Solicitor in Rabaul, we suffered another burglary. Quite early the next day, a large truck arrived at our premises carrying about 30 or 40 members of the Duk-Duk. They assured me that they knew who was responsible for the burglary and that they were on their way to deal with the matter and invited me to travel with them.

I told them I didn't think it was necessary for them to do such a thing and that I certainly did not feel that in my position as Deputy Public Solicitor for the New Guinea Islands, I could be involved in any matter of the sort they had in mind.

They departed, I think a little disappointed with me.

I think that they must have shown significant restraint because the next thing I knew was that a number of contract labourers from the New Guinea Highlands had presented themselves at the police station and confessed to the crime. Obviously, it was not necessary or appropriate that I act for any of them and so I never found out what took place. It was, however, obvious that there was a value attached to being a member of that society.

There had been riots in Rabaul in December 1969. My Tasmanian friend, Kerry Dillon[1], had been in Rabaul at the time of those riots and has written something of them himself.

I arrived in time to pick up the conduct of a few trials that arose from those riots. They had been, as far as I could tell, largely symbolic events with very little in the way of injury inflicted on anybody.

By the time the riots came to trial, they had been largely resolved in the village by payments of compensation and many of the Crown witnesses seemed to have developed selective loss of memory as to what had happened.

I appeared in a few of the trials and as I recall things, very few people were ever convicted of anything.

The picture below was taken on the steps of the original Rabaul Courthouse where all the Court work was conducted until the new Court was finished, just in time for the commencement of the Emanuel trial.

---

1   See Kerry Dillon – The Chronicle of a Young Lawyer (2020)

With John Griffin and Sean Flood and some prominent members of the Mataungan Association on the steps of the Rabaul Court House – recently acquitted men not robed.

Another cause of significant ill feeling in the Tolai community was the imposition of a head tax. This was thought to be a clever move by the administration to raise funds for the conduct of something resembling local government.

The problem was that the Tolai people lived in villages and were largely self-sufficient and the villages were not to receive anything by way of services or assistance for the payment of the head tax. Not surprisingly, they elected not to pay it.

Many of them were arrested, no person more prominent than the member of Parliament for East New Britain, Oscar Tamur. Oscar was arrested on the instructions of the then Crown prosecutor in Rabaul.

I was told that he was in police custody and I went to the courthouse to see him (see photograph below).

Sean Flood had an idea that Oscar's case could be resolved by the making of a habeas corpus application.[1] Both of us were familiar with the principal but had never been involved in such an application before.

We decided that the basis of the application should be that, as Oscar was a member of Parliament and had been on his way to the airport to travel to Port Moresby to attend the Parliament, he could not be arrested and therefore should be delivered to the Court, where he might be released. The picture shows me having a conversation with Oscar at the Rabaul Courthouse concerning the legal principles involved.

With Oscar Tammur at the Rabaul Courthouse

---

1 Habeas Corpus is a recourse in law through which a person can report unlawful detention or imprisonment to a Court and request that the Court order the custodian of the person, usually a prison official, to bring the prisoner to Court to determine whether the detention is lawful.

The application was successful.

Oscar was released.

The Tolai people in general and in particular, the Mataungan Association members were delighted.

Sean Flood presenting the Pubsol Oscar to Norris Pratt (prosecutor) after the successful habeas corpus application

Christine with Berenat (holding John) and Gineveppa

The Emanuel Trial – Rabaul

Errol John Emanuel was murdered at Kabaira plantation on 19 June 1971. At the time, he was the District Commissioner (the senior administration person) for the East New Britain district.

The murder excited strong feelings in and around Rabaul. The Tolai people regarded Emanuel as a traitor to them. That was because he had been involved with them many years before assuring them that some land that had been taken away from them during the German administration of the Gazelle Peninsular would be returned to them and later he was sent by the Australian administration to inform them that the administration had changed its view and as a result, the lands would not be returned.

It was a very insensitive thing to do because any thinking person would have realised that the Tolai people saw every action as personal and did not really comprehend the difference between personal views and government actions. Emanuel had been very popular both in the expatriate community and with the Tolai people until this decision was taken.

Feelings in the expatriate community ran high because, consistently with the Tolai view that Emanuel was a traitor, he was put to death by being stabbed with a Japanese bayonet, somehow left over from the Japanese occupation during World War II. It was an awful way to die and an awful thing that Anton ToWaliria (who was a young and inexperienced man) was the one delegated to do the stabbing.

At the time the murder occurred, I was living in and working out of Port Moresby. Peter Lalor asked me to return to Rabaul to organise the defence of those who were charged. There were originally 24 accused but after a committal proceeding, only 18 were committed for trial. The Crown elected to proceed against 14 of those committed. The trial, which commenced in Rabaul on 12th February 1972, ultimately proceeded against 13 because one of them had been unrepresented at the arraignment.

The evidence against each of the accused consisted largely of confessions made to police officers. Eight of the accused challenged the admissibility of those confessions and evidence was heard on a voir dire.

The trial Judge rejected one confession in its entirety and admitted six others in full and one in part. The Crown offered no further evidence against the man whose confession was rejected in its entirety. The trial before The Chief Justice of Papua New Guinea, Justice Minogue, attracted an impressive cast of lawyers from Australia and Papua New Guinea.

FG Brennan QC (later Chief Justice of the High Court of Australia) (with him N Pratt and C Wall) appeared for the Crown.

JW Galbally QC (with him JP Barry (later to become a Family Court Judge) and later T Martin QC (with P L Sein) appeared for the accused, William Taupa ToVarula

EA Lusher QC (with KJ Carruthers) appeared for the accused, Anton ToWaliria.

KJ Carruthers also appeared for the accused, Thomas ToGogol.

P Luke appeared for the accused, Joseph ToMarum.

PJ Moss appeared for the accused, Tomano ToVolo.

R Wood appeared for the accused, Lekius ToPait.

J Hartigan appeared for the accused, Francis ToPulumar.

J Hamilton appeared for the accused, Aron ToLiplip.

M Adams appeared for the accused, Tomas Painuk.

E Pratt appeared for the accused, Otto Kaliop.

M Morris appeared for the accused, Clement ToVavaula.

S Flood appeared for the accused, Joseph ToVuvu.

The trial continued over 79 sitting days. On 16 June 1972, five of the accused were convicted and on 20 June, those convicted were sentenced to various terms of imprisonment.

My role in the trial, indeed in all of the proceedings that led up to the trial, was to act as solicitor for all the accused except William Taupa, who was initially represented by the lawyers arranged and funded by the Mataungan Association, an association formed by local people dissatisfied with the payment of head taxes and believed to have been closely associated with the planning of Emanuel's murder. The association had little idea of how much lawyers from Australia would cost and soon ran out of money and Taupa was forced to make an application for legal aid, which was, of course, granted.

Nobody expected that the trial would take as long as it did, and I left Rabaul in early May to get married and thereafter took only a minimal part in the completion of the trial. My part in the proceedings was really finished because all the evidence had been given, all the necessary instructions had been taken and argument and submissions were what was remaining. My principal contributions had been in the taking of instructions because I could speak pidgin English better than anyone else involved.

The trial was another truly fortunate part of my life because I spent those three months in the company of some very experienced and incredibly talented lawyers.

In his Reasons for Judgment dated 16 July 1972[1], Minogue CJ found five of the accused guilty of wilful murder – Taupa as one who aided, counselled and procured the commission of the crime, ToWaliria as the one who fatally stabbed the deceased and ToMarum, ToPait and Kalip as persons who aided in the commission of the offence. The remaining accused were found not guilty.

Taupa was sentenced to imprisonment with hard labour for 14 years, ToWaliria for 11 years, ToMarum and ToPait for two years each and Kalip for 18 months.

I have always thought of it as an incredibly significant triumph for the defence. One also had to admire the performance of the Chief Justice who was able to remain calm and dispassionate notwithstanding the incredibly significant provocation offered him by the lawyers involved.

In an article in the *Australian Financial Review* of 24 June 1972, it was said of the trial:

'The notoriety of the trial stems from its cost in money and professional skills, its length (nearly five months) the revelations of police irregularities in interviewing

---

1   Regina v William Taupa Tovarula and others 1973 PNGLR 140

suspects and holding them without charge - criticised by the Chief Justice in his summary - allegations of police brutality by defence counsel and the extraordinary zeal with which defence counsel raised so many points of law on behalf of their clients.

It is said here that the legal system itself has been on trial'.

'Several weeks of the trial were consumed by submissions from counsel for and against the admission of confessions obtained from the accused by the police.

Professor O'Regan advocates that all confessions be admitted and that it be left to the Judge to decide how much weight he accords them.

Opponents of that reform, including one law lecturer at the university, Mr Jack Goldring, and a Supreme Court Judge, argue that this would encourage police to obtain confessions at any cost by fair means or foul'.

John Baulch QC

Michael Adams, John Hamilton, Richard Wood, Brian Hoath and John Hartigan

Oscar Tammur

I had been admitted as a Barrister and Solicitor of the Supreme Court of the Territory of Papua and New Guinea for a little more than three years by the time the trial concluded and I count myself very fortunate to have been involved in it because there was so much to learn from the senior lawyers who attended to represent the accused. When I returned to Australia in 1974, I still felt that I was a little ahead of people who had similar seniority in the profession to my own. It was almost all due to participating in that trial.

Even with serious litigation like this going on there had to be lighter moments. I mention three.

The first involves me. The Emanuel trial was conducted with the assistance of interpreters who had been obtained from a religious college on the New Guinea mainland. It seems that they did not understand too much about pidgin English, though they were said to be experts.

One of the continuing problems in dealing with pidgin speakers was the use of the expression *kilim*. That word was commonly used to mean 'hit'. *Kilim e dai* meant to hit somebody so that they fell down. *Kilim e dai pinis* or *kilim e dai pinis olgeta* meant to kill somebody in the sense in which an English speaker would understand it. The mission-trained interpreters demonstrated time and time again that this distinction was lost on them and as the defence team's best pidgin speaker, I became increasingly frustrated with them.

This led me to write a note concerning the use of these words and how they might be used to promote the replacement of the interpreters with people who understood what was going on. The note was certainly not intended for general circulation but shown by me to two clerks then employed in the Public Solicitor's Office who assisted in instructing all the counsel conducting the defence.

During the lunch hour, somebody (and I suspect I know who) extracted the note from my file and left it at the prosecution end of the bar table where it somehow came to be shown to the mission interpreters. They were, I suppose not surprisingly, outraged.

For reasons that I cannot now recall I was not at the court when it resumed but I know that the *Post Courier* newspaper of 29 February 1972 reported that one James Parker, a Court interpreter, said he had been disturbed by a note circulating in the court during the lunch break. Peter Luke, then Deputy Public Solicitor and counsel for one of the accused, described the note as 'the jottings of an idle mind' and took it upon himself to apologise on behalf of 'another person'. It was not suggested to me that I should apologise to anybody and I would not have done so.

It did not seem to me at any stage that any legal person involved in the trial other than me had the concern that caused me to write the note – that the interpreters were not up to the job.

The interpreters however, I think, got the message because several of them became unavailable and by 8 March 1972, the shortage of full-time interpreters was threatening to bring the trial to a halt (see the *Post Courier* newspaper of 8 March 1972).

I accept that in the current politically correct environment in which we live the first thought anyone would have had would have been to apologise to somebody about something without thinking about whether there was a serious issue. But I was a little surprised that what I had intended as a humorous way of drawing attention to a serious problem never penetrated the thought processes of those involved in the trial.

I am not sure what happened to the note. If I had it, I could reproduce it here in the interest of making it clear to readers what my views are about robust communication of ideas about serious issues.

The second incident involved one Kevin McCreanor, who was charged with being in a dwelling house without lawful excuse. The newspaper of 24 February 1972 recorded that the police were forced to close the case against the law student without the principal witness giving evidence because she was late, notwithstanding that it was known that she was being brought from the nearby Duke of York Islands by speedboat. She arrived at the Court just a few minutes after the police had been forced to close the case.

Mr John Hartigan, a Sydney barrister, appeared on behalf of the law student, who must've counted himself somewhat fortunate as it appears from the newspaper article that he alleged that he had gone to the women's dormitory of the United Church hostel in Rabaul at 1:00 am on 25 January to return some keys – the property of a motel – to a waitress who resided there. A likely story.

A third incident involved a Public Solicitor's Office lawyer named James Fingleton, who pleaded not guilty to a charge of behaving in an offensive manner after walking about naked in the restaurant at Kulau Lodge, on the north coast road outside Rabaul. It emerged that Fingleton had removed his clothes and gone for a swim and that another of the defence team had taken his clothes and hidden them. The whole thing was, it seemed to me, just a storm in a teacup but, because of the high feelings that were aroused in Rabaul by the trial, assumed great importance.

The person who complained was a schoolteacher named Pamela Barker who had been in the restaurant at the relevant time and asserted that the alleged offender 'stood near her'. She was quite unable to explain why she chose the following morning to make the complaint to the special branch, which would not normally have been interested in such a thing.

In a decision commendable for what I would call a common-sense approach, the Magistrate, Mr Mitchell, found Fingleton had behaved in an offensive manner by walking about as alleged but discharged him without conviction.

At the other end of the behaviour scale, the leading prosecutor at the Emanuel trial, Mr FG Brennan QC (later Chief Justice of the High Court of Australia) attended mass daily, often driven by CF Wall, who was not then and never has been since, as far as I'm aware, well-known for attending mass.

All in all, the Emanuel trial was a great experience for all those involved and firm friendships were forged. Several reunions have been held in the years since the trial concluded and they are invariably well attended.

Return to Port Moresby – May 1972

As mentioned above, I left Rabaul before the conclusion of the Emanuel trail and returned to Port Moresby.

I was soon involved in another difficult case involving two Goilala men charged with the wilful murder of an eight-year-old girl. It was a shocking crime and not surprisingly, attracted some very bad behaviour by the investigating police.

The Queen v Peter Ivara and Kasimilo Guraea

Trial Judge: Mr Justice Kelly

Trial date: 5 July 1972 to 7 August 1972

Sentence: 30 August 1972

Peter Ivara, aged 32, and Kasimilo Guraea, aged 22, both Goilala men from the Central district, were charged with the wilful murder of Avilapa Laiam, aged eight years. It was alleged that the two men had taken the girl from outside the Hohola cinema to an area of bushland opposite the Port Moresby rifle range, raped her and killed her by striking her repeatedly with rocks.

Guraea had apparently come to the girl's mother's house late on 11 November to stay the night. The mother awoke early in the morning and, finding her daughter missing, asked Guraea if he had seen her. She said that he'd replied that she was not in the house and that they had gone to Ivara's house, woke him and began searching for the child. Her body was eventually located by Ivara in the company of police. She was naked, covered by branches and leaves, and surrounded by bloodstains.

Both men made admissions to the police.

Mr friend, Brian Hoath (later Queensland District Court Judge) was briefed to appear for Ivara, and I was briefed to appear for Guraea. This short summary of it will indicate that the case was not an entirely straightforward one from a defence point of view.

In what is known as a 'voir dire' proceeding, I challenged the admissibility of the admissions said to have been made by Guraea. I did that based on the instructions that Guraea had been struck on a number of occasions by two different police officers, stripped of his clothing and made to stand on one leg for a significant period of time before being interviewed by Inspector Hodder.

I also alleged that the accused – Guraea – had a poor understanding of the pidgin English language in which his record of interview was conducted.

Inspector Hodder, during a challenge, denied:
- That labels on the evidence bags reading 'shorts removed from Kasimilo' and 'shirt removed from Kasimilo' confirmed Guraea's allegation that his

clothes had been removed from him at the Boroko police station

- That he had recorded the interview in English so as to produce a document that was his interpretation of what was said
- That he had intentionally asked 'loaded questions'

The *Post Courier* newspaper reported the outcome of that proceeding on 17 July 1972. Mr Justice Kelly rejected allegations that Guraea had been slapped on the face or hit on the back of the head or made to stand on one leg.

Mr Justice Kelly did, however, accept that Guraea's shirt and shorts had been removed from him at the police station before the record of interview had been conducted but said that he was satisfied that that had not been done forcibly. He went on to say, 'The removal of the defendant's clothes may well have caused him some discomfort or embarrassment ... but it did not constitute a threat.'

Mr Justice Kelly did not, however, exclude some questions and answers from the record of interview.

This result was more than a little bit disappointing to me because it seemed to me that Inspector Hodder's denial that the clothes had been removed, combined with prison officers' evidence that Ivara had arrived at the prison without any clothing following the record of interview, justified a rather more robust finding about what had gone on at the police station.

Brian Hoath, on behalf of Ivara, also made an unsuccessful challenge to the admission of the confessional evidence led against him. This was a significant obstacle to his defence because the admissions led against Ivara included admissions that he and another man (presumably Guraea) had decided to have sex with the girl and kill her so that she could not tell her mother and father.

Mr Justice Kelly ultimately accepted that evidence and found Ivara guilty of wilful murder. He found Guraea not guilty of wilful murder or murder, but guilty of manslaughter. He said of him that he had been present while the girl was killed and 'offered no opposition although he had the means to do so'. I thought this a somewhat curious finding having regard to the age disparity between them.

The distinction between the offences of which they were convicted was of importance because only a conviction for wilful murder could result in a death penalty being imposed, while a conviction for manslaughter could have resulted in no more than life imprisonment.

Sentencing was delayed for a period so that further information could be gathered about Ivara's background. Almost a month later, he was sentenced to 15 years imprisonment and Guraea was sentenced to five years imprisonment.

Guraea's woes were not over. When the trial finished in Port Moresby, I returned to Rabaul, leaving the consideration of an appeal to others in the Port Moresby office of the Public Solicitor. Sometime later, I heard that advice had been taken from senior counsel in Brisbane who said that in his opinion there was no prospect of success in any appeal on Guraea's behalf. While I thought this was curious, I was busy enough with other work and did not make it my business to seek a detailed explanation.

It was only years later that I spoke with the counsel in Brisbane who had been asked to give the advice and he told me that he had not been asked to give any consideration to the question of the admissibility of the confessional material.

The case was a great lesson for me about the need for a person to have conduct of a matter from start to finish rather than to have it passed around in an office for retention by different people at different times.

While it can probably safely be said that Guraea was a man 'not burdened by the weight of merit' in his defence, I would have felt more comfortable if all avenues had been explored.

The Queen v Katia, Abauwa, Kapero and Pelia

This trial took place in Port Moresby during the interval that elapsed between the convictions of Ivara and Guraea and their sentence.

Trial: 16 August 1972 to 25 August 1972

Sentence: 30 August 1972

Trial Judge: Chief Justice Minogue

Defence Counsel: Hoath (Katia), Baulch (Abauwa), Broadley (Kapero) and McMaster (Pella)

This case was not interesting for any legal point or any great forensic argument but simply because of an unusual outcome.

The four men had been charged with the murder of another man during a fight that began in a tavern and finished on the road outside.

The trial took place before the Chief Justice in Port Moresby. Once again, I have drawn on newspaper reports to supplement my memory of how things went.

The trial lasted a few days and, beyond the variances that would be expected in a case of this type, the evidence emerged as fairly consistent in respect of each of the four accused. By the time it came to addresses, I imagine the Chief Justice was finding the whole thing a little tedious.

My address commenced after lunch and after a short time, I noticed that the Chief Justice appeared to be asleep.

I looked enquiringly at my fellow defence counsel, hoping for some useful advice about what I should do. Broadley said that I must make an effort to wake him up perhaps by tipping over some books or a water jug or something of that sort and that seemed like a good idea.

So I knocked over a pile of books. The Chief Justice woke up and shook his head. I told him I had reached the end of my submissions. He thanked me and went on to hear other addresses.

I was very surprised to find that when the verdict was announced, the chief justice indicated that he was not satisfied that any of the men were guilty of wilful murder but three of them were guilty of manslaughter. The man I represented was acquitted altogether. I really think that that occurred only because the Chief Justice was concerned that he might not have heard some critical part of my submissions. It certainly was not because of some superior forensic skills that I displayed during the trial at its conclusion.

It's an example of what my friend RD would call 'superior ring craft'.

The French Girls

On the waterfront at Madang with Uris Laucis and our French actresses.

Uris Laucis, Crown Prosecutor, and I travelled to the Sepik district to conduct trials up and down the Sepik River.

Whilst in Madang, we met a film producer from France, who was making a film in the area. He was very good company in the evenings. One evening he informed us that two of the actresses he was travelling with had been arrested by the police and charged with indecent behaviour.

I told him that if they were not good English speakers, they would need to think about being represented when they appeared in Court. He told me they couldn't speak English at all. I told him that if that was the case, the public solicitor could appear for them and because I was the Deputy Public Solicitor for the islands, I could grant them legal aid.

With the assistance of the producer, I had a short conversation with each of the actresses, utilising my schoolboy French and his very good English. They were very happy about being represented by the public solicitor and so was the producer, as I recall things. We drank some champagne to seal my engagement.

It became apparent that the girls had become the subject of attention on the beach because one of them was in the nude altogether and the other was wearing what came to be known as a thong.

I had a conversation with Laucis and told him that it seemed to me that there might be a conflict of interest between the two girls because whether or not one could be said to be behaving indecently by being naked in a public place, it might be a rather different question as to whether or not one could be said to be behaving indecently if one was in a public place wearing a thong.

He was keen to be involved notwithstanding that it appeared that the charges had been brought at the instigation of Superintendent Thomas (a very important policeman in the district – at least in his own opinion).

I went to Court that next day with the producer and the two offenders and told the Magistrate that there was a difficulty in proceeding with the case quickly as while I was able to use the producer as an interpreter, the Court would need to find an interpreter proficient in French and English to translate the proceeding as the girls would be pleading not guilty.

This caused a little consternation.

It was arranged that the proceeding would be adjourned until the last day of the circuit when it was expected that all the other cases would be finished.

Back at the hotel that evening, I was enjoying a quiet drink with Laucis when the superintendent arrived. He told me aggressively that he wanted to speak to me concerning this case.

I told him that he should speak to Laucis as well because Laucis would be appearing for one of the girls when the matter was resumed at the end of the following week.

I found Laucis and we met again in the bar.

By that time the superintendent had become a little agitated and he told us in no uncertain terms that it would probably be a complete waste of time for us to return to Port Moresby (he did not know that I came from Rabaul) because neither of us would have a job by the time we got there.

Laucis was a little concerned about this but I told him not to worry as everything would be fine (I was then of the view that there was no way that the police could or would incur the expense of getting a French interpreter).

The superintendent departed.

The following morning, a police officer of junior rank appeared at the hotel to deliver a telegram to me. He told me that he had been directed by the superintendent to go and collect the telegram and to bring it to me at the hotel. How it came about that the superintendent knew that there was a telegram for me and I didn't was never explained.

I told the police officer that I would open the telegram at breakfast time when I would be in company with Laucis and we would discuss what, if any, response was necessary. The police officer told me he had been specifically instructed to wait and to take any response back to the superintendent.

I told him the only place to wait was down in the breakfast room, which is where he went.

I met Laucis at breakfast and told him that I had a telegram from the public solicitor, and I wondered whether he had received any communication. He said he had not.

In his presence, I opened the telegram. The message was brief. It read:

Baulch – please ensure that official receipts are issued in respect of any contributions received for legal assistance.

Lalor.

The police officer approached again and enquired about whether he could take a response to the superintendent. I gave him the telegram and told him he should hand it to the superintendent and tell him that I did not need to make any response.

Laucis (who I think had been a little concerned about what the reaction from our superiors in Moresby might be) was greatly amused.

Needless to say, by the time we returned to Madang at the end of the circuit, all the heat had gone out of the matter. The police prosecutor told me that he was instructed to withdraw the charges and that is how the matter finished.

It was Laucis's idea that we should adjourn to the waterfront and have the photograph taken. I am glad we did because otherwise the matter might have been forgotten.

Christine

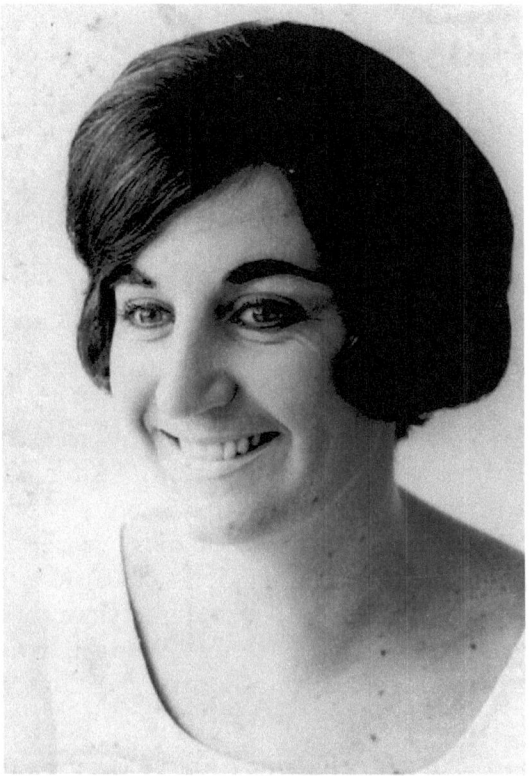

Christine and I met in Rabaul in 1970. Christine was working with the Treasury Department in Port Moresby. We met through an old friend of hers who had become a friend of mine while I was living in Rabaul. She was travelling about Papua New Guinea with her mother and so I met my future wife and future mother-in-law on the same day.

It was not a great start to our relationship because it had been arranged that I would escort the two of them to a ball in Rabaul, where my friend was an escort for one of the debutantes, but I went to sleep for a time in the afternoon and consequently arrived to collect them rather late. Notwithstanding that, our relationship blossomed and Christine said that she would arrange a party for me to meet the people in Port Moresby when I came over there.

True to her word, she did just that. Sadly, I was sleeping when the party began and once again arrived late.

It was a very good party and I'm not sure that it would have been a good idea to arrive early because I don't think that even in those days, I had the stamina for partying that Christine and her friends displayed.

Anyway, we were obviously getting along fairly well as by the end of the year we were both entitled to holidays. (To explain – we were contracted by the Australian Government to work a two-year term. After 21 months we were entitled to three months' leave and were flown to the capital in Australia, from where we departed). We went to Sydney (where we decided we would get married the following year in Port Moresby) and then to Tasmania (where Christine met my parents). We undertook a tour of Tasmania in a rather dilapidated car that my sister loaned us. It was a good time.

We returned to PNG just after Christmas, each of us having signed a further two-year contract which, as things turned out, would be our last.

We married at St Mary's Catholic Cathedral in Port Moresby on the 13 May 1972 and honeymooned in the British Solomon Islands and had a most enjoyable time there. We stayed at a hotel in Honiara for a time and then at a coastal resort run by a partnership between expatriates and the local population. It was a wonderful, relaxing time at the resort and every evening our meal was accompanied by entertainment provided by some of the expatriates and the local population. We enjoyed it greatly.

We were also able to obtain passage on a small coastal vessel to travel all around the British Solomon Islands and we saw some very interesting sights and met genuinely nice people.

The difference between the British administration and the Australian administration in PNG was very apparent. Most of the Solomon Islanders that we met spoke English quite fluently. They were also very friendly and outgoing.

Pat Shanahan and Nick Cowdrey and an acquaintance (in the blue shirt) on an island off the coast of Rabaul

With Stella Rumet and her child

Chrissie and I with our boat in Rabaul Harbour – typical weekend activity.

Other Pacific Islands

The Solomon Islands

After enjoying my visit to the Solomon Islands in 1972, when I was asked to return to the Solomons to defend a police officer, I jumped at the opportunity.

Jeriel Ofea Ausuta was charged that 'on a day unknown between 26 July 1972 and 31 January 1973, in the Protectorate, being employed by the public service of Her Majesty as a Senior Inspector of Police, stole a wristwatch valued at $30, which came into his position by virtue of his employment.'

When I arrived in the Protectorate, I was met at the airport by Jeriel and several of his friends who were also senior members of the police force. It emerged that there had been a very large storm in mid-1972 and all police had been on duty continuously for some days. I was told that in the course of the response to the emergency, Jeriel had obtained a watch from the lost property basket because he did not have a watch and needed one to perform his duties.

When the emergency was over, he had placed the watch with other clothing and equipment in the locker assigned to him at the Honiara Police Station. It was discovered during some sort of audit early in the following year and he was charged with stealing it. He believed, his friends believed, and I came to believe that there was some sort of stunt going on that was designed to result in him being demoted.

I went to see the prosecutor, but he was immovable.

I went to see the magistrate to enquire about dress and was told that shorts and a short-sleeved shirt with a tie would be sufficient.

'Sufficient'. When I arrived the next day, dressed as advised, I sat in the court for a short time before the magistrate appeared in shorts, no socks, sandshoes without laces and a shirt unbuttoned to a little above the navel.

This bloke has been having a lend of me, I thought.

I cannot recall the outcome of the hearing. I imagine it must have been a not guilty finding. The defendant and his friends took me out to dinner that night. Both sides were satisfied with the outcome.

We dined at a local Chinese restaurant and the dinner seemed, to my recollection, to be a celebration victory.

Trip to Kiribati

At the beginning of 2001 I was, like many others, I suspect, completely unaware of Kiribati. I did not know where it was, how big it was, how to get there, what happened there or anything else.

An old friend from PNG rang me and asked if I would be interested in travelling to Kiribati and conducting an appeal in the Court of Appeal there. The Court of Appeal, he told me, was comprised of judges from New

Zealand. The case was a case that he had conducted on behalf of a native of Kiribati concerning a dredge called *The Nautilus*. My friend had been there the previous year and conducted the initial litigation before a resident Judge who was a South Australian before he took up his appointment in Kiribati.

I was a little intrigued because I thought I knew a fair bit about the Pacific Islands, but I had never heard of this place. A little initial research told me that it was located near the intersection of the equator and the international dateline. It consisted of eight or nine islands, all quite small.

Things were a little quiet in Townsville when he rang me, and I thought why not go and have a look at this place? Being a lawyer, I wanted to be sure that there would be appropriate financial arrangements in place.

This was the first problem. It seemed the client was able to raise enough funds to fly me to Kiribati and accommodate me but the payment of fees would depend upon the outcome of the litigation, as *The Nautilus* was his client's only significant asset.

I asked him to send me the material so that I could give the matter some thought. I was cautious because my old friend was not famous as a successful litigator.

I was met at the airport by the woman who claimed that she was the owner of the barge *Nautilus* and she took me to a comfortable motel. I began to think that things were looking up.

Another error. There was much worse to come.

A housemaid employed by the hotel came to my room when I was in the course of unpacking. She observed that I had laid out on the bed a snorkel, goggles and flippers. (I had brought these items with me, thinking that they would help me fill in the time in what would otherwise be a fairly tedious stay in a very hot place in the Pacific). She enquired whether I intended to go swimming in Kiribati. I told her that I did.

'You must not do that,' she said. 'You will get very sick.'

This was disappointing news to me, and I pressed her about why she thought that would be the case. Eventually, she was able to explain to me (overcoming some reluctance to discuss topics of this type with a white stranger) that because of the absence of the sewerage system it was the practice of villages to empty their toilet buckets into the sea and that although the water looked very nice it was not suitable for swimming.

Fortunately, Mary (my client, the owner of the motel and the owner of a hire car business) had provided me with a hire car so I was not completely without the means to entertain myself while I waited for the appointed Court day.

It took about half a day to drive over all of the passable roadways on the island and, having done that, I was lucky to find a club used by expatriates and local people in the afternoons for a social drink and a very friendly Attorney General, who not only approved my application to practice in Kiribati but also invited me to join him for morning tea on more than one occasion.

It is interesting to look back on that period and recall that there was one area on the island to which I could not gain access. That was said to be a 'watching post' owned by the Chinese Government and built entirely at the expense of the Chinese Government. Looking back, I suppose, that was the beginning of Chinese interest in the Pacific Islands.

I visited the Chief Justice. He was a very nice man from Adelaide, but he was also the man whose decision I was to support in the appeal hearing so my communication with him was necessarily limited. He did, however, give me some useful information about things to do.

I visited a small war museum containing relics from World War II. Those relics were very interesting. There was also some film involving what I was told was the first amphibious landing by American troops. The landing did not go well because the landing craft ran aground some distance from the shore and the American troops suffered significant casualties just getting ashore. When they did get ashore, the Japanese occupiers retreated to tunnels that had been dug in the hills and the Americans dealt with them by pouring petrol into the tunnels and setting fire to them. This was shown in the film, which had the very appearance of being genuine rather than fabricated. It was quite horrific to watch.

When the day of the appeal arrived, it was the usual unbelievably hot day in Kiribati. I had arrived at court early, as was my usual practice, to find that the air conditioning did not operate well or at all and that all available fans had been placed on the bench for the comfort of the judges and that none were available at the bar table.

I enquired as to the status of the air-conditioning. The Clerk of the Court assured me that the air-conditioning was on and functioning at maximum efficiency. I pointed out to him that it was 29 degrees at the bar table and very humid. He said to me that that was exactly what was to be expected because it was 34 degrees outside and so the air-conditioning was operating well.

Desperate times give cause for desperate measures. I left the Courtroom and went to the room provided for counsel, where I took off my robes, removed my shirt and singlet and replaced my jabot, bar jacket and gown over the otherwise naked torso.

I returned to court. My adjustments to my clothing did not seem to have been helpful. While my Indian opponent was making a long address in support of the appeal, one of the Judges noted my discomfort and suggested that I might be more comfortable if I were to remove my gown and bar jacket. I assured him that this would not lead to me presenting a pleasing sight to the court. He smiled in a knowing way, leaving me to think that I was not the first person to encounter the sort of difficulties that I have related.

The hearing of the appeal proceeded as well as could be expected and, when the decision was given some weeks later and in my absence, my client was successful in every aspect except the one which had never been mentioned in the Court of Appeal or the course of the argument.

By the time the decision was given, it was clear to me that I was not going to be paid beyond the initial payment that I received on account of expenses.

In addition to the adjustment, the judgment was something like $5,000 in $150,000 and I imagine that the clients were happy to accept that rather than approach me again to discuss the prospect of appeal, which would have involved discussing my outstanding fees.

It was, however, an interesting exercise and one which I will never forget. While I was unpaid, I was not out of pocket, and I was also one of few people I know who ever visited Kiribati. So I do not regret it.

When I returned briefly to Papua New Guinea in 1986 (to appear for an expatriate man charged with raping a local woman), I travelled to Mount Hagen.

The case was over and the expatriate was acquitted (on a technicality concerning the way in which the investigation had been conducted) in a short time. Shortly after that, I encountered the same Tolai police officer who I had acted for in Rabaul, in the street in Mount Hagen. He obviously had not sought discharge from the police force as we had discussed and was occupying a very senior position in the Western Highlands District.

He offered to take me on a tour of Mount Hagen and its surrounds, assuring me that such a tour would be a good thing for more than one reason. First, it would improve my knowledge of the area and second, it would improve my prospects of staying safe in Mount Hagen if people saw me riding about in a motor vehicle with him.

I was happy to accept his offer but a little surprised when he obtained his vehicle from the police station. It was necessary for me to sit in the rear seat of the Toyota

Landcruiser because there was no front passenger seat. The area where the front passenger seat might have been contained a gun rack with four or five rifles and shotguns, in addition to the pistols that he wore on his belt. There was no glass in the windows of the vehicle, but iron bars covered all of the spaces where the windows had once been.

While he was driving me about, he told me something about his day-to-day work. It was no doubt dangerous and from time to time involved setting fire to the homes of the local population. He explained that taking such a course brought peace to the area for at least as long as it took for the people to rebuild their homes.

I could not help thinking about the way in which his methods mirrored the methods of patrol officers operating in Papua New Guinea prior to World War II.

PART 4
Townsville, Queensland

In 1974, we left Papua New Guinea between self-government and independence. I had worked in Papua New Guinea with Eamon Lindsay. He had returned to Australia and taken up practice as a solicitor in Townsville with his brother, Richard. He contacted me on a number of occasions, urging me to come to Townsville and practice in his firm (Lindsay and Lindsay) as a solicitor.

I had also spent time with Judge Shanahan, who served as a Judge of the National Court of Papua New Guinea for a period of some months. Judge Shanahan had spent some time in Rabaul, where he not only presided over many cases in which I was involved but also spent some time with Christine and me socially. He sang the praises of Townsville and I was later to learn what a significant influence he had been at the Bar in Townsville prior to his appointment as the District Court Judge based in Rockhampton.

A third consideration, which is rather odd looking back on it, is that Christine and I were a bit concerned about the climate we would return to. We did not want to find ourselves in a place that was too cold. As time went on, we often laughed about that.

We arrived in Townsville in February 1974 and I commenced work with Eamon and Richard Lindsay straightaway.

My introduction to the judiciary in Townville was in the Magistrate's Court. The magistrates were a Mr Murrell and Mr Henderson They had to be seen to be believed.

A word of explanation.

My very first attendance at the Magistrate's Court, then located in what is now the Townsville Little Theatre building, was at Eamon Lindsay's request, to receive a judgment in a civil case. The judgment was to be delivered at 2:15 pm. Being new in town, I arrived a little early, sought directions as to which Courtroom (there were two) might be the appropriate one and went and sat in the back of the Courtroom.

There were no lights on and no one else about.

I sat for a while in the back of what appeared to be the major Courtroom and after a time a man appeared, turned on the lights and arranged some books, stamps and the like on the bench. He was dressed rather like a tram conductor and I took him to be the Clerk of the Court. I was quite wrong. After a time, he returned and ascended to the bench as a police sergeant led a number of Aboriginals into the court.

Mr Murrell sat down as the sergeant arrived at the prosecutor's position at the bar table.

Mr Murrell looked at the prosecutor and said, 'Yes, sergeant?'

The prosecutor replied, 'All drunk, Your Worship,' making a general gesture with his right hand towards the Aboriginals.

Mr Murrell enquired, 'Previous?' And the sergeant began to hand up a series of documents which I took to contain a record of the prior offending of each of the assembled Aboriginals.

Fresh from my New Guinea experience, I thought I should help. I stood up and moved to the Bar table, told the magistrate my name and said that by way of offering assistance to the court, I wished to point out that none of the Aboriginals had been asked whether they were guilty of any offence.

The magistrate responded, 'You act for them, do you?'

I replied, 'No, Your Worship, I just thought that I would assist the court by pointing out what seems to me might be said to be a defect in the proceedings.'

He responded, 'You could assist the Court by sitting down and remaining silent.'

I did.

Each of the Aborigines was fined ($2.00 each, as I recall) and escorted from the courtroom. The Magistrate then commenced to give the decision that had brought me to the Magistrate's Court.

When I returned to the office of Eamon Lindsay and Richard Lindsay, I recall having a discussion with the partners about the similarities between Court practice in Townsville (as demonstrated by this story) and what we had thought to be the fairly primitive Court practices that prevailed in Papua New Guinea.

Worse was to come.

I had occasion to appear before Mr Henderson both personally representing clients and instructing counsel on behalf of clients. It did not seem to me that it made any difference whether counsel was engaged or not – it was extremely difficult for anyone seated at the Bar table other than in the location reserved for the prosecutor, to engage in any meaningful discussion with Mr Henderson.

During counsel's addresses or defending solicitors' addresses, he would commonly set aside his pen and take up a stamp, which I came to know was the stamp that was applied to the court file to record a conviction and the penalty.

On one occasion, a barrister that I was instructing declined to continue his final address 'until Your Worship tells me which stamp it is that you are holding.'

Mr Henderson threatened the barrister with contempt.

The barrister, who had plainly been there before, pulled a chequebook from his suit pocket and enquired how much that would cost. There followed an uncomfortable silence which ended eventually when Mr Henderson put down the stamp and invited counsel to continue.

As instructing solicitor, it seemed to me that things were not going all that well. It turned out I was right. When the client was convicted, the barrister asked me whether I had the Notice of Appeal prepared. I had not. He seemed to think that a little odd. As time went on, I came to understand that it was a good practice to have a Notice of Appeal ready to file when one was doing any business in the Magistrate's Court in Townsville.

I do not know how many times I went straight from the Courtroom, where the client had been convicted and sentenced to imprisonment, to the Clerk of the Court's office to lodge a Notice of Appeal and have the client admitted to bail.

It was a depressing business but necessary.

During my time in Townsville, there was an appeal (in which I was not involved) heard in Brisbane in which Mr Justice Douglas of the Queensland Supreme Court was reported as having said of one of the Townsville magistrates 'the town must live in fear of this man'.

I am sure that it did. Fortunately, things got better with the passage of time and there was much better to come in the superior Courts and as my familiarity with the profession grew.

Durward, Davey, Lafferty, Pope, Baulch, Pearce, Dr Gavin Douglas, Turnbull. Note: Davey and Dr Gavin Douglas were not members of RJ Douglas' chambers.

The Judges in Townsville

The Judges in Townsville at the time were Sir George Kneipp of the Supreme Court and VJ Finn of the District Court.

VJ Finn was an interesting Townsville character. Prior to his appointment as a Judge of the District Court of Queensland, he had been a prosecutor in Townsville for many years. I never saw him prosecuting but I am told that he had a great way of communicating with juries. I am not surprised to hear that because he certainly, as a judge, demonstrated a great ability to deal with juries in a way that made them feel part of the system rather than victims, as I am sure that some jurors felt when they were in court with other judges.

Sir George Kneipp saw himself as a leader of the profession and particularly as a leader of the Bar and I pretty quickly came to understand that the barristers practising in Townsville also saw him as the leader of the Bar. He was a very talented lawyer and also a very generous and kind man. He was always ready to assist a barrister struggling with a difficult case, a difficult point or plain lack of experience.

There was a lot of work to do in Townsville but the interesting thing was that in the late 1970s, members of the profession still found time for collegiate dinners and special events.

I cannot now count the number of dinners that I attended to celebrate anniversaries of practitioners' admissions. I fear that all of that has disappeared now as the profession is not a friendly and collegiate group.

Some funny stories

Flowers for Lady Kneipp

I visited Sir George Kneipp at his house one afternoon on the day that the Law Ball was to be held.

I found His Honour sitting under the house as I think he was often given to doing, and he invited me to join him there and offered me a large bottle of beer. We sat and talked about how the evening would progress because he was required to make a speech.

While we were talking, a florist arrived with a bunch of flowers. He was aware that he was visiting Sir George's house and so was somewhat cautious in the way he approached the property. He could see us seated under the house and he called out, 'I have flowers for Lady Kneipp.' I knew that these were coming because the organising committee of the Law Ball had arranged for that to happen.

Sir George, who could produce an impressive booming voice when he wished to, called back, 'Flowers for Lady Kneipp? Oh, good. Would you take them upstairs? They might improve her mood.'

Later, I came to know the florist quite well and he told me that he would never forget that delivery. I won't forget it either.

The Lost Dog

Another story that was told about him is, I think, probably untrue, but nonetheless a very funny story.

It is said that he was found outside the hotel in one of the less salubrious parts of town looking somewhat distressed. Those who found him enquired as to whether they could be of assistance. It is said that His Honour told them that his dog had gone into the hotel.

For the Term of my Legal Life

Someone suggested that he should just go in and get him. His Honour is said to have replied that he couldn't do that because the clientele of the hotel included many people who had seen him in Court.

That same resourceful person said that he should just stick his head in the door and call the dog. It is said that His Honour laughed and said, 'I couldn't do that.' When asked why, he explained that the dog's name was Nigger.

PART 5
A Brief Return to Tasmania

I applied for the position of second-in-charge of the Australian Legal Aid Office in Hobart. My friend, Kerry Dillon, was the officer in charge. Kerry was involved in the opening of the Hobart branch.

This is my recollection of a case while in Hobart.

Brett Howard Lynch was acquitted by Hobart magistrate Mr Brettingham-Moore on 24 February 1976, on charges of having assaulted a Detective Sergeant Robert Geoffrey Fielding by pointing a loaded pistol at him and having been in possession of an unlicensed pistol.

The acquittal resulted in the suspension of three officers involved in the evening, Detective Sergeant Anthony Henley, Detective Sergeant Robert Geoffrey

Fielding and Detective Constable Reginald John Wells. It also resulted in charges of assault, perjury and attempting to pervert the course of justice being brought against the three suspended officers.

The trial commenced in Hobart on 21 July 1976 before Mr Justice Neasey. I appeared for the prosecution, led by Mr Roger Jennings QC, and Mr MG Everett QC and with him, M. Brian Morgan appeared for the accused police officers.

The case concerned events that occurred in a massage parlour, Caesar's Health Studio, Victoria Street, Hobart. The prosecution case depended upon the evidence of a Mr Lynch and was supported by a tape recording that appeared to support his version of events.

The three officers had arrived at Caesar's between 9:00pm and 9:15pm on 24 December 1975. Lynch said he saw them arrive through a peephole in the office door. He said he immediately turned on a cassette tape recorder under the reception desk. The tape recording supported Lynch to the extent that the detectives said they would search the premises and did so before one of them 'bid him farewell' and said, 'All right, thanks very much Mr Lynch for your trouble,' before Fielding was heard to say, 'You are now under arrest for assault.'

The issues had all been litigated in the Magistrates Court, of course, so there was knowledge by both sides of what the other side would say. The defence case was that Lynch had produced a pistol and Fielding had disarmed him and then arrested him. The problem with that was the tape recording revealed no sound of a struggle before Lynch was arrested.

Jennings QC, opening the case for the prosecution, said the authenticity of the tape was the central issue.

The Crown case concerning the authenticity of the tape was not insignificant because, at about 2:00 am on Christmas day, Lynch's sister-in-law had been to Caesar's and removed the cassettes from the tape recorder after receiving a phone call. She said that she played it twice at home then wrapped it in Christmas paper and put it under the Christmas tree.

At 8:30 am on Christmas day, she called a Mr Fabian Dixon, a well-known Tasmanian lawyer, who played the tape twice before giving it to his lawyer father, Mr JH Dixon, who then sealed it in an envelope and locked it in his strongroom.

On 8 January 1976, the tape was handed to another lawyer, Mr Peter Underwood, (later the Chief Justice of Tasmania and later still, the Governor of Tasmania) and he played it to Mr Lynch for the first time.

Lynch said his arrest came out of the blue and denied producing any pistol. He said he was punched in the stomach after being told that he was under arrest and bundled out of the door and down the stairs where he was repeatedly punched and kicked, before being taken to the Hobart police headquarters.

He said that while in the vice squad room, Fielding had approached him with a gun and said, 'This is the gun you assaulted me with tonight. It's a formidable gun, isn't it?'

He said he was urged to take hold of it but he declined.

Lynch said he asked to be taken to hospital because his shoulder and his collarbone were sore. He said he was taken to a toilet where he cleaned blood off his face and was told to clean up the basin. He was then taken to the charge room and then to the Royal Hobart Hospital through a side door. He said that after receiving treatment at Hobart Hospital he was taken back to the charge room and then locked in the police cells.

He said that at 8:00 am on Christmas day his brother and Mr Fabian Dixon saw him in the cells and he was granted bail by a Justice of the Peace.

He said that the cassette recording was not played to him until two or three weeks later when Mr Peter Underwood played it to him.

Lynch admitted that 'relief massage' had been provided at Caesar's. He said that by 'relief massage' he meant masturbation. He denied being aware that any of the girls who worked on the premises had sexual intercourse with the customers. This was not the most believable part of his case.

Lynch had been removed from the premises at about 9:30 pm on Christmas Eve so the opportunity for anything to have been done with the tape was between that time and 2:00 am on Christmas morning. There was an inconsistency in the evidence in that Lynch said that the tape had been left under the counter of the reception desk while his sister-in-law said that when she arrived to collect it at 2:00 am, it was in full sight on top of the counter. Lynch's brother gave evidence that he picked the cassette up from under the reception desk and put it on the desk before his wife took the cassette out. He said it was under the front desk 'where it usually was'.

Mr Underwood gave evidence.

He said that he heard of Lynch being arrested sometime between 9:00 pm and 9:30 pm on Christmas Eve. He said that he had recalled receiving a phone call from one of the suspended detectives between 9:00 pm and 9:30 pm and was told that Lynch was in their custody and had been taken to hospital. He spoke to Lynch on the phone before catching a ferry into the city and walking to Caesar's Health Studio. He tried to get in but the door was locked. He said he saw blood in a 'substantial, wavering line from the building along Victoria Street to the junction with Harrington Street'.

He said that he went to the police station, where he spoke to Lynch for a few minutes. He noticed there were injuries to his nose, there was a gash on his left upper temple, impressions of bruising about his face and blood all down his jumper and all down his trousers. He confirmed that he had received the tape from Mr JH Dixon in January 1976. Mr Underwood had conducted Lynch's defence in the January hearing in the Magistrates Court.

An interesting piece of evidence concerned the doctor at the Royal Hobart Hospital. He gave evidence that he had seen Lynch on the evening in question and that he'd been brought to the hospital by three detectives.

He said that he asked Lynch what had happened and he refused to answer, making gestures that he could not talk because the police were immediately outside the cubicle. He said that he asked the detectives to move so that he could talk with Lynch, but they refused to do so.

He said he found a laceration on the forehead, a bruise to the top of the head and a bruise over the collarbone. He said there was also evidence of blood loss over Lynch's clothes and shoes, which could have come from a nosebleed and the gash.

A doctor from the Royal Hobart Hospital gave evidence. He said the injuries were consistent with being struck by fists or pushed around and falling on hard objects.

A police officer from the ballistics section gave evidence that the gun Lynch allegedly pointed at Sargent Fielding was a Smith and Wesson revolver. He said it had no serial number, the numbers having been removed in several places. Another police officer said no fingerprints were found on the pistol.

A senior technician at the Australian Broadcasting Commission had investigated the tape. He was one of the Crown's last witnesses in the case. He surprised all by saying not only that he was concerned as to whether or not the tape had been edited but that the possible edits were at critical positions on the tape.

It was curious indeed that this never came up before because all of these issues had been canvassed in the Magistrates Court. Be that as it may, it certainly suited the defence case because following the calling of that witness, defence counsel was able to open the case for the accused man and indicate that the tape expert from Russell Street Police headquarters in Melbourne would be called to give similar evidence about the editing of the tape.

The trial was adjourned so that everybody could go to Melbourne (at the Crown's expense) for this investigation to be pursued.

Not surprisingly, further investigation at the Russell Street Police Station confirmed the view of the witness who had been called on behalf of the accused.

Qualities not previously noted on the tape were unearthed in Melbourne and notwithstanding the fact that there seemed to have been little or no opportunity for anybody to carry out the sophisticated work of interfering with the tape, my leader was persuaded that the only appropriate course was not to proceed further on the indictment. I must say I had some reservations about that but I was a very junior prosecutor and my views were not sought on the matter.

Later, as I became more experienced, I thought it a good thing that usually preparation is done in advance of the trial rather than on the run during the trial.

Many cynics thought that the result had more to do with who the accused was than with the rights or wrongs of the case. My friend, JD, a salesman, used to say that 'proper preparation prevents poor performance' and I think that is a rule that should be remembered by all who have anything to do with serious litigations.

PART 6
Return to Townsville

We returned to Townsville in 1977 towing a trailer that held our most treasured material possession. The station wagon had our three-month-old daughter, Justine, on the back seat and our two Irish setters in the rear.

James Oswald Hunter, then a barrister, decided he wanted to move to Bowen and own a mango property. He and his family did this and Jim then practiced as a solicitor in that town.

This then left a vacancy for me in Townsville as a barrister at the private Bar. This is what I had decided was what I really enjoyed the most.

Some Interesting Queensland Cases

1. The Hughenden circuits
2. The Bowen circuits
3. The Patterson family

The Hughenden circuit was a significant part of my practice in my early life at the Townsville bar.

I had first been to Hughenden in my capacity as a solicitor and instructing Robert Pack of Counsel (RD to his friends). Others involved included Judge Finn and a Mr Peter Elliott, the judge's associate, then referred to as the judge's clerk.

Judge Finn was a hard-working judge who also enjoyed a bit of fun out of court. Upon learning that I'd had to leave my vehicle in Hughenden on a previous circuit and was proposing to bring it back at the end of the next sittings, he proposed that he, RD, Peter Elliott and I should travel back in the car together. This sounded good to me.

I did not realise until the trip was underway that His Honour proposed to introduce me (as the new boy in town) to every licensed establishment between Hughenden and Townsville. There were plenty of them in those days and we stopped at each one, only for one drink, but by the time we had reached Charters Towers in the late afternoon, I had to tell His Honour that I did not feel that it was safe for me to drive the vehicle any further that day.

Far from being disappointed, His Honour seemed to welcome the news, suggesting that I should drive to the Excelsior Hotel where we could stay the night and he would introduce me to Mrs Fitzgerald, the publican. He sang Mrs Fitzgerald's praises, telling me that at some suitable time, she would show me around the hotel.

Accommodation was confirmed ($10 per night for a single room) and we enjoyed a few convivial drinks in the main bar, one of those large horseshoe-shaped bars, where Mrs Fitzgerald sat at a cash register in the middle of the room and the barmaids poured and delivered drinks and delivered payments and received change from Mrs Fitzgerald at the till.

When trade slowed down, Mrs Fitzgerald offered to show me around the hotel. We went upstairs and I saw a sample of the rooms that we were to stay in that night. Each one had a single bed, a small wooden wardrobe and what appeared to be a brand-new hand basin in the corner.

Each of the rooms opened off a large communal area but also had French doors opening onto the veranda outside so that air-conditioning was not required as there was good cross-flow ventilation.

Doing my best to make conversation with the elderly Mrs Fitzgerald, I enquired whether the hand basins were as new as they appeared to be. She told me that they were – installation of them had very recently been completed. I enquired whether she thought that the provision of a hand basin in the room when there were adequate communal bathrooms at the rear of the building would provide any significant additional attraction and/or income for her.

She looked at me curiously, and after a few seconds said, 'I don't know, love, but I hope that it will stop the ringers pissing in the wardrobe.'

A significant silence followed as I was quite unable to think of a suitable response.

RD became the life and soul of the party on subsequent trips to Hughenden. He had an engaging sense of humour and was given to purchasing a bottle of port ('luggage') almost every day, explaining that it was a suitable way to finish the meal. He would pull the cork from the port bottle with his teeth and spit it out the window, saying, 'We won't be needing that anymore.'

I cannot remember an occasion when we did need it again. What I can remember is a rather startled look on the face of more than one judge who witnessed this introduction of the 'luggage'.

RD was not finished with one of the judges yet. A few months later, we travelled to Bowen to appear at the trial of two young soldiers charged with respect to a little escapade they had had in a military Land Rover. They were charged with unlawfully using the vehicle after it was involved in an accident on the outskirts of Bowen.

One of them informed the police that the accident was in no way due to any fault by the driver but was due to the sudden appearance of a black dog in front of the vehicle. The fact that it was black was relevant because the accident occurred at nighttime. Somehow, RD was able to persuade the judge that it would be appropriate to take the jury on a view of the scene of the accident.

Off we went, the judge, his associate, the Indian prosecutor, RD and I in one car and the jury in a specially chartered bus.

When we arrived at the scene there was what seemed to me to be some fairly pointless wandering about looking at the road surface and edges, before quite unexpectedly, at least from my point of view, a black dog appeared on the scene. RD asked the judge to point out to the jury that there was a black dog on the scene. The Indian prosecutor was apoplectic. The judge declined.

The soldiers were ultimately acquitted. My impression was that the jury had an idea that the whole thing was a bit of a joke. The Indian prosecutor told us before we left the courthouse that he thought that RD and I were 'very tricky fellows'.

The trips included an introduction to the Patterson family as well as an introduction to the intricacies of jury selection in small communities. Those two subjects, as it turned out, were closely connected.

The Patterson family owned (by virtue of grazing leases) very substantial areas of property not too far from Hughenden. As I understand it, they were amongst a number of families who adopted the practice of always eating the neighbours' cattle rather than their own. To provoke the neighbours, the hide of the butchered animal would be hung over the boundary fence so that the neighbour, when doing his rounds, would know that another beast had been taken.

Members of the family assured me that there was nothing too provocative about this because the neighbours behaved in exactly the same way. Whilst I never saw any evidence of it, I have no reason to disbelieve what I was told.

When I was visiting Hughenden later in my capacity as a barrister, I was approached by the bailiff on one occasion and asked if I could intervene in respect of the execution of some Warrants of Execution which were required on the Patterson property. He asserted that the Patterson family had told him that he should not come onto the property because he would find himself at the bottom of an old mineshaft, where rescue would be unlikely.

With an eye at least, in part, to future briefs in the area, I thought it safe to stay out of this. I did, however, on one occasion, mention it to one of the Patterson family and recall that person affecting a somewhat injured air and saying, 'Oh, Mr Baulch, you don't think that any of us would say something like that, do you?'

Enough said.

Sadly, the Patterson family were later victims of the rapacious banking practices of the time and I think that the Westpac bank ended up in possession of most, if not all, of their property.

There are some stories about that family related to incidents in the Hughenden District Court that are worth relating.

I recall an occasion when one member of the Patterson family was charged with wilfully damaging a hay bailer that belonged to a competitor in the hay bailing business.

A relevant piece of evidence was an axe that had been located in the rear of the accused man's utility, which, the police alleged, showed traces of red paint matching the red paint on the damaged hay bailer.

The axe became an exhibit.

The defence proposed to call evidence from a couple of likely lads associated with the Patterson family. I should pause to mention that the Hughenden District Court sat in a room in which there were lots of windows. Those whose attention was not riveted by what was happening in the courtroom could see what was happening outside.

During the course of the defence case, it became apparent to the bailiff and a number of the jurors that one of the lads was dealing with a snake that had emerged from underneath the courthouse. It was a very large black snake and while the likely lad in question managed to get the heel of his western boot onto its head, his position was still somewhat precarious as the snake had wrapped itself around his right leg and the snake's tail was somewhere about the level with the lad's hip.

The bailiff went outside to investigate. He returned, requesting that he be permitted to take the axe that I have told you about outside to assist in disposing of the snake.

The judge, somewhat unfortunately named Judge Hanger, declined his request in case the use of the axe to dispose of the snake resulted in the loss of valuable evidence.

By now, the attention of almost everyone in the Courtroom was on the lad and the snake rather than what was happening in the courtroom.

The bailiff left the Court again to explain to the lad that the axe could not be used by him. He returned after a short period and was able to relieve the tension by advising that the lad had been able to kill the snake by rotating his heel on its head.

It seemed to me that the only matter that interested the jury from that point onwards was the lad and the evidence he would give.

An acquittal followed a brief retirement of the jury.

Another member of the family found himself under investigation over an incident said to have occurred on the Hughenden/Richmond Road at night after a session in the hotel.

It appeared that this family member had got into an argument in the hotel and had left alone in his utility to travel home. He became aware that he was being followed by two vehicles, each occupied by a number of people.

Never short on resourcefulness, he stopped his vehicle in the middle of the road so that it was necessary for those following to get out of their vehicles and walk to him. Whilst they were doing that, he noticed they had armed themselves with what appeared to be baseball bats. Reaching under the seat, he retrieved his Magnum 45 pistol but kept it out of sight.

He then produced the pistol and remarked to the nearest man, 'You c****s are mad. You've come to a gunfight with sticks.'

Police became involved. They were delighted to inform me that during the course of a Record of Interview, the relevant Patterson had told them that he didn't care what they charged him with because his response would be to get the German c**t to attend Court and another acquittal would follow.

The police took great delight in recording this response and making sure that it was referred to more than once in the balance of the conversation with him.

So excited were they that they forgot to ask any questions that might have negated the obvious defence of self-defence and further forgot to ask any question that might have been relevant to the question of whether or not the pistol (which was licensed) was being carried in an appropriate way in the motor vehicle prior to the incident.

The Fun We Had

While in Townsville, I took to writing some poetry (doggerel), which I recited at the regular bench and bar dinners that were held in the 1980s. I include a few of them, not seeking praise as a poet, but just as an indication of how good those times were.

1981 End of Year Recital

> *The law is practised in the North*
> *by men of style and skill.*
> *We all understand their worth,*
> *for any barrister will tell anyone at any time*
> *the story of his skill.*
>
> *Our reputation in the South*
> *is second now to none.*
> *They pass the tales by word of mouth,*
> *how northern cases are won.*
>
> *Let us pause now to assess*
> *the good works that we've done,*
> *the suffering alleviated*
> *in nineteen eighty-one.*
>
> *There have been times we've come unstuck,*
> *instance a while ago,*
> *the man tried for attempted rape*
> *seemed very keen to go*
> *to prison where he might reflect*
> *On the consequence of moral neglect.*

John Baulch QC

We sent him there with quick dispatch,
but Justice, alas, was tricked.
In such a rush we sent him off,
we forgot to take the verdict.

Then came the terrible day
the rotter appealed to the CCA,
and far from sparing his victims pain,
they said it must be tried again.

But we stick to tradition here in the North.
Cullinane sets the example,
for he understands what a brief is worth,
and whether the fee is ample.

He deals with difficulties with ease,
this year in Cairns take note,
he had two Judges to try to please,
five briefs on the day to tote.

We'd see him there at nine fifty-five,
outside the old Cairns Court
to settle, adjourn or sometimes strive
to get what he knew he ought.

He was never in fear or faint of heart,
for when disaster was at hand,
two briefs: two Judges: five minutes to the start,
he was able to call on Land.

So Land set off at furious pace,
his robes from his case he prised,
ran all the way back but arrived that day,
to find the case compromised.

For the Term of my Legal Life

Paul Cosgrove has seen action too,
in Townsville's police Court,
defending a case in which he knew
that the prosecutor ought
be fair and show him all they had.
Paul found their conduct terrible bad,
so bad as to be quite beyond belief,
when they tried to steal his precious brief,
they tugged and pulled and swore.

The brief was being damaged;
Paul sought to appeal to the law,
but the Magistrate had vanished.

Now Paul reflected on that act
at length with furrowed brow,
and reached a decision reflecting tact
not to let the matter grow,
but rather that, it fitted
that the terrible man,
who authorised the plan,
should in fairness be acquitted.

And when after a unanimous vote,
the Bar association battled,
by law to grasp the constable's throat,
and shake him until he rattled,
the commissioner, in whom we trust,
ruled Cosgrove's decision impeccably just.

So now Martenns, who took the brief,
looks on Paul with awe,
'I stole his brief like a common thief,
and still he didn't get sore.'

John Baulch QC

This year we lost a valued friend,
not lost to us but to the law.
we thought his reign would never end,
but while in Bowen, Judge Finn saw
his time approaching, his day near done,
when setting out for a little fun,
escaping from Ron Smith and me,
the good Judge befell injury.

For Vince was sportsman to the core,
appreciating all he saw,
and when in Bowen on circuit,
no sporting interest did he quit,
but spent his time at his best sport,
as a talent scout for Playboy *ought,*
and roamed the streets at every chance,
giving all girls a glance.

Alas, the good Judge was brought undone
one day while roaming in the sun.
The air was warm, the day divine,
he never even saw the sign
that was so clear to all of us,
announcing where to catch the bus.
Head averted, some young girls to greet,
he crashed into a bus stop seat.

Poor Judge with severely injured shin,
away from home, from kith and kin,
he never doctor or nurse sought,
although Bob Penman said he ought,
for he could see through all the pain,
he might be called on to explain
the cause of his new malady
to his unsympathetic lady.

For the Term of my Legal Life

And Mrs Finn still ponders now,
and asks occasionally just how
this injury occurred to Vince.
she is not fooled by the fact that since,
when he goes bowling with the lads,
he solemnly straps on shin pads.

Now as my tail burns down to its embers,
come the sporting achievements of one of our members,
for Baulch's eleven chosen to play
at the rugby club last Saturday.
The night was warm, the match under lights,
when Webb, forsaking his Superman tights,
appeared at the ground for the cricketer's rights,
resplendent in most magnificent whites.

Sent in to bat in difficult light,
the profession team faltered at first that night,
then Webb strode to the pitch with nonchalant air,
none would have guessed he was on a pair.
The clerks were downhearted just at the sight
of Webb swinging the bat with all his might.

He cut and pulled and gave his all,
and once he even struck the ball,
but age caught up, as it's bound to do.
Webb retired exhausted at the score of two.

There was rejoicing by the clerks,
and by the nature of their remarks,
they thought they had it truly won,
it seeming to them that Webb was done.

With the clerks batting and going well,
I come to the best I have to tell,
for just when they seemed on their metal,
our Webb, their plans was to unsettle.
They gave an impolite derisive howl
when he came to the northern end to bowl,
but they were to see the start of the rout,
on his second delivery came a runout.

In the field to Webb gave an impressive display,
holding the only catch taken that day,
but alas, Webb is retired, no more will he play,
for after the game he evinced some dismay,
and said that he wouldn't do things so risky
had he known before play on that Saturday,
that Judge Finn had not donated the whiskey.

And now as we go to our well-earned vacation,
let's present a united glum face to the nation,
and pray these tales never are told,
lest it be when we are all very old,
for if it ever gets out that we
find our work funny,
our customers may prove hard to
part from their money.

Don Cleary was a prominent member of the Townsville legal profession and a partner in the firm Boulton Cleary and Kern (earlier Nehmer, Boulton Cleary) before moving to Brisbane and establishing a firm Cleary and Hoare. When he left Townsville, an outrageous party was held at the South's rugby league club, wherein keeping with the nature of the evening, I recited this poem.

Don's Parting

Don Cleary is a country lad,
A country lad made good.
Now he's off to the big smoke,
as one day we knew he would.

Before he goes, we'll pause a while,
his achievements to consider,
and then we'll offer him for sale
to the highest, if any, bidder.

For Donald has of recent time,
been a person of some note.
I'll tell you now of that in rhyme,
and put him to the vote.

For the Term of my Legal Life

He was articled in clerkship,
as lawyers mostly are,
he suffered the deprivation
of drinking in public bars,
but he had friends who helped him out,
in one of them was Mahon.
Alas, he lost Mahon's friendship
by reneging on the shout.

Poor Mahon had gone to the men's room
when it was Cleary's turn to buy.
Poor unsuspecting Mahon – of drinking beer not shy,
who on returning raised his glass,
and drank to Cleary's health.
He coughed and choked and cried foul wine,
for he had been caught by a fearful rort,
in his glass was some Cleary urine.

Now gentle listeners do not feign
disgust or think this pointless,
for humans learn by experience
and none more so than Cleary.
He always keeps his glass nearby
and is of toilets leery.

Well, Don became a lawyer then,
and set out to develop
a practice that would beat the rest,
and good clientele develop.

With this in mind, he bought a boat,
a beautiful machine.
He meant to show all kinds of men
what being his client could mean.

Now Cleary was the captain,
in charge of the whole show.
He meant those clients to maintain,
and so, set off to go
to Radical Bay,
just for the day.

John Baulch QC

*Little thinking then,
that many's the slip
twixt cup and lip
with Cleary at the helm.*

*Well, the Beryl K sank that day,
leaving not a trace.
The day was clear, and the sea was calm,
you'd think Cleary would lose face.*

*But Cleary demonstrated then,
the qualities that make
heroes distinct from mortal men,
when he set out to take
what could be salvaged there,
and saved for his guests' sake.
He struck out for the sinking ship
while others stood in fear.
That day he showed himself the boss
by rescuing the gear,
lest he have had a total loss,
although she was insured.*

*When Cleary returned from that hazardous journey,
which all knew had been very risky,
he brought not the log, the food or the money,
but the esky of beer and the whiskey.*

*Alas, all else was lost that day,
it's my sad tale to tell,
but the captain and crew
went straight away
to the Radical Bay Hotel,
for Cleary knew they had work to do.
They could leave nothing to chance
for on getting home they had to go
straight out for the insurance.*

For the Term of my Legal Life

*Now plainly Cleary did it well,
this post-mortem of the wreck,
for when they came to tell the tale,
there was not any speck
of evidence that could gainsay
the total loss of the* Beryl K.

*And it's been said by a gossipmonger,
that though his guests that day had thought
that Cleary's boat was a little short,
for insurance it was longer.
Not only did insurers pay
for motorboat and gear,
the insurers had a terrible day,
for they paid for the whiskey and beer.*

*But Cleary's life's not been all fun,
he's had to do some things serious.
He had a talk with Lindsay one day,
and made the poor chap quite delirious.*

*For Don was maintaining that lawyers beware
and charge a proper fee,
lest we encourage that terrible day
when lawyers will be free.*

*He voiced his cause with force that day,
poor Richard looking pensive.
He couldn't get a chance to say
that what concerned him in a way,
was that he thought Don inexpensive!*

*You see, Don was a man of many parts.
He likes his beer, music and arts,
but of all his ventures one in memory sticks,
I speak of his entry into local politics.*

*He gained endorsement in a team
of independent nature,
they thought the council right off-beam,
and lacking in real stature.*

John Baulch QC

Well the race was run, and the counting done,
and our poor Don defeated,
and he'll always say to his dying day,
how was my deposit estreated?

We have all tried to explain,
and thereby to allay Don's pain.
It's like having a bet on the tote
with the great big donkey vote.

It can't be a sin
to be found second-best
in an even contest,
but our efforts have all been in vain,
for Don is convinced in a quite settled way
that lawyers on council have a big part to play.
what sticks in his throat
is the popular vote that said that one lawyer is ample,
and faced with the choice,
in unanimous voice,
said give us Ms Delma Benson.

In his newfound abode,
when his courage has growed,
Don will no doubt stand again.
And his friends when they meet him,
with kind voice will greet him,
and never breathe dear Delma's name.

Well, now you all know why our Don has to go,
why for him there can be no returning,
but shed not a tear for somehow, I fear,
for his friends now and then he'll be yearning.

Now when Don grows old
in the South's bloody cold,
and begins to feel life's full fatigue,
may he think of the night,
of the extraordinary bunfight,
held at the South's rugby league.

Webb (the altar boy), Cleary (Superman) and the author (policeman) at Don's parting. A police prosecutor loaned me the hat and the police shirt but drew the line at loaning me a baton. Because of that I had to make do with a carving from Papua New Guinea, which you will see, aroused Cleary's interest.

The substitute police equipment came in quite handy because I was called upon to eject some gate crashers during the evening. They were already so inebriated that they did not observe that the policeman ejecting them not only had a painted face but also a rather unusual baton.

I have located many other poems that I wrote and recited at various times. None of them can be included here because we live in a different world where a robust disposition and unrestrained laughter are sure signs of impropriety. So those who were present on the occasions of my other recitals will have to live with just the memory.

On one occasion I recited this in Court. I include the transcript below in case you doubt me.

(Issued subject to correction upon revision.)

IN THE DISTRICT COURT HELD AT TOWNSVILLE

CRIMINAL JURISDICTION

BEFORE JUDGE HALL

8 FEBRUARY 1985

(Copyright in this transcript is vested in the Crown. Copies thereof must not be made or sold without the written authority of the Chief Court Reporter, Court Reporting Bureau.)

- - - -

THE QUEEN -v- PAUL KEITH BENNETT

NOLLE PROSEQUI

Mr Durward, (Crown Prosecutor) for the Crown.
Mr Baulch, (instructed by L.R. Middleton, Esq, as town agent for the Public Defender), for the accused.

MR DURWARD: I mention the matter of The Queen against Paul Keith Bennett. There is an indictment before the Court charging him with manslaughter of a feline. I might add that the matter has been considered - that is the depositions - and we did receive a subjective opinion from Mr Baulch about the matter. I say "subjective" because he is a dog owner and the Deputy Director, who gave consideration to the matter, gave an objective assessment because he is both a cat and dog owner. Apparently I am being asked to do this because Mr. Irwin's name appears on the indictment, as I understand, and I think he though it fitting that I should also be recorded in posterity as having my name on the indictment somewhere. I ask for the return of that indictment.

HIS HONOUR: You are standing in as his deputy?

MR DURWARD: Yes - deputy deputy.

(Indictment handed to Mr Durward).

MR BAULCH: While my learned friend is doing that, I should tell Your Honour that this may be the first example of the new operation of the prosecution's section under the Director of Prosecutions. Yesterday, from the newly appointed Deputy Director of Prosecutions, I received a letter in which he was waxing lyrical about this case and inviting me to come here and I felt I should not let the occasion pass without reading the content of the letter into the record. Omitting the formal parts it says:-

-1-

For the Term of my Legal Life

> "Tomorrow we will all go to court
> On a matter exceedingly short
> Concerning a cat carnivorous and fat
> Shot dead for devouring a bantam.
>
> The Accused was committed for trial
> Prosecutors inspected the file
> Shall he stay where he are and be tried at the Bar
> Or go free this assassin most vile?
>
> But the Accused need not now be chided
> For the Crown has quite definitely decided
> That the demise of the feline is not even a small crime
> For the slaughter on seeing his bantom get ate
> Is protected by Section Four - Fifty eight."

I am instructed that is correct - s 4-58 would have applied had this matter gone to trial.

HIS HONOUR: Could you make that letter available to the reporter? He was probably not able to record it at that rate. You "purred along" quite nicely.

MR DURWARD: If it had not been for Mr Baulch denying responsibility for that letter, I would have sworn it had a certain style about it that I have heard at bar functions previously. I return the indictment endorsed appropriately.

(Indictment handed to His Honour).

HIS HONOUR: What an appropriate course. The accused is discharged.

- - - -

PART 7
Things that Mattered

The Queen v Brian Marlin

Brian Marlin was a detective based at Mackay when I first met him. I had the impression that he was a very conscientious police officer, not afraid of hard work.

When it came about that he was charged as a result of enquiries made by the Fitzgerald Inquiry, he asked Gene Paterson if he would ask me to act on his behalf. Gene and I had done some work together and our relationship was to become much closer as a result of acting for Brian Marlin over a protracted period, which eventually resulted in the Crown electing not to proceed further on the indictment against him.

There were many things that happened during that trial which left one with little confidence in the way in which the Fitzgerald Inquiry had been conducted and the way in which subsequent prosecutions were conducted. It does not seem necessary to set it all out now. Suffice to say that Gene and I became good friends as a result and that friendship persists until this day.

It is worth spending a little more time on the Marlin case.

Background

Brian Marlin was born on 2 October 1944.

The front page of *The Courier-Mail* on 21 July 1977 (coincidentally the same month that I was admitted to practice as a barrister in Queensland) reported that 37 probationary police constables would take part in an induction ceremony the following day.

The paper informed readers that Brian Marlin had been a detective in New South Wales and had resigned to become a bylaw inspector with the Redland Shire Council in 1970 before joining the Queensland Police Force.

Brian took his oath the following day (22 July 1977) and the document was witnessed by the then Commissioner of Police, Terry Lewis.

In 1980, Brian completed three subjects run by the Department of Education Queensland – Queensland Police Administration (Honours), Police Law 1 (Credit) and Business Communications 1 (Credit).

It was the practice in the police force that an authorised commissioned officer would prepare a report about each serving officer at designated intervals.

On 1 December 1980, Detective Superintendent Murphy said of Brian:

An extremely active former Criminal Investigator. Resourceful in ideas with a rare ability to efficiently use informers and persons in the criminal twilight arena.

On 16 December 1982 Detective Superintendent Doull said of Brian:

The Detective Senior Constable is a valuable member of the Upper Mount Gravatt CIB and will, no doubt, make a competent NCO at some future stage. He is hard-working and efficient and his far better than average results reflect his ability. He is suited to CIB duties and should prove of increasing value in the future.

On 18 August 1983, Detective Superintendent Robertson said of Brian:

An efficient hard-working investigator of above average ability.

On 26 October 1984, Inspector Daniels said of Brian:

A keen, intelligent and reliable officer who has proved his outstanding capabilities as an investigator. He has been responsible for the clean up of a number of major incidents in this District. He is hard-working and efficient and will make a competent NCO.

On 7 July 1986, Inspector McMahon said of Brian:

The Detective excels in licensing and consorting type of work. It has been as a result of this type of work that much criticism has been levelled at him from both within and outside the Department. I have yet to see any such criticism validated.

Detective Marlin also has the ability to investigate all types of criminal offences including those of a complicated nature.

There were apparent difficulties in him being unable to work in harmony with other staff but I have seen a vast improvement in this area during the past 12 months both from him and the other members. I feel that I have established good communications with him and it has been pleasing to have him approach me, discuss work problems and seek my opinion on many matters. I further feel that he is a person who, if one is prepared to have faith and confidence in, will not let you down.

He does not take excessive sick leave.

On 28 August 1986, Inspector Plant (of Mackay) said of Brian:

This detective is a good all-round investigator. He is dedicated, conscientious and very active in the field of criminal investigation. He also exhibits expertise and enthusiasm in licensing and consorting duties. His work output is excellent.

He does not take unnecessary sick leave.

In 1984, whilst based in Mackay, Brian passed the exam qualifying him for the rank of sergeant second class.

I have set out all of these matters (perhaps in a somewhat tedious way) because they provide a useful background to understand what came next.

By late 1987, the Fitzgerald Inquiry had subpoenaed the Queensland Police Credit Union Ltd and the Commonwealth Bank of Australia to produce records relating to Brian and his wife. Brian did not know of this until advised by the financiers and his request to the Department of Justice to be supplied with copies of the documentation met with the response that he should pursue the matter with Commissioner Fitzgerald QC who was conducting his enquiry independently of the Queensland Government.

In January 1988, Brian was requested to supply to the Commission all notebooks and diaries compiled by him in and after 1 January 1977.

On 2 February 1988, Brian was interviewed by Andrew Philp and Ross Martin, officers of the Crime and Corruption Commission Queensland.

On 5 March 1988, Brian was interviewed by Gary Crooke and Ross Martin, officers of the Commission.

On 8 March 1988, the *Daily Mercury* (Mackay newspaper) reported that Brian was suspected of shooting the pet dog of a police inspector and it was said that that allegation had been made to the Fitzgerald Commission on the previous day. Curiously, this allegation had not been raised with Brain at either of his interviews with Commission staff.

On 10 March 1998, the *Daily Mercury* reported that a retired officer named Wilby had said that Marlin had told him that he was going to shoot himself because he was depressed after being departmentally charged over the alleged pistol-whipping of a man at the Cleveland Sands Hotel. The man was said to be an associate of Tony Murphy. Again, curiously, this allegation had not been raised with Brian in either of his interviews with Commission staff.

On 11 March 1988, the *Daily Mercury* reported evidence given at the Commission to the effect that Marlin threatened to kill another officer (the evidence was given by an Inspector Dautel). Yet again, this was an allegation that had not been raised with Brian during either of his interviews with Commission staff.

The significance of these matters is doubtful in any event. However, what is and remains a very curious feature of the whole investigation is that these matters were not raised with Brian, particularly in view of the close proximity in time of the interview he had with Commission staff and the calling of the evidence that led to the publication of the allegations in the newspaper.

On 17 August 1988, a warrant was issued for the arrest of Brian Rodney Marlin on a charge that :

On a day between the 14th day of January and the 1st day of May 1987, at Mackay in the State of Queensland being a person employed in the public service as a Detective Senior Constable of Police in which capacity he was concerned in the prosecution of offenders, corruptly received a sum of money, namely $2,000, in consideration that he the said Brian Rodney Marlin would, with a view to corrupt, interfere with the due administration of justice, omit to do his duty in respect of an investigation into the theft of a quantity of cigarettes.

This was to be the start of one of the longest and most drawn-out cases that I was ever involved in. Fortunately, from my point of view, as well as from Marlin's point of view, the prosecution was ultimately unsuccessful.

There was a committal proceeding in respect of that charge and two other charges:

- 'That on a date between the 5th day of August 1986 and the 30th day of September 1986 at Mackay, in the State of Queensland, Brian Rodney Marlin being a person employed in the Public Service as a Detective Senior Constable of Police in which capacity he was concerned in the prosecution of offenders, corruptly received a sum of money namely $2,000, for himself on account of his, the said Brian Rodney Marlin, having with a view to the facilitation of the commission of an offence by one Michael Paul Falzon, supplied information to the said Michael Paul Falzon.'

- 'On or about the 6th day of August 1986 at Mackay in the State of Queensland Brian Rodney Marlin being a person employed in the Public Service as a Detective Senior Constable of Police in which capacity he was concerned in the prosecution of offenders, corruptly received a sum of money, namely $5,000, for himself in consideration that he, the said Brian Rodney Marlin would with a view to corrupt interference with the due administration of justice omit to do his duty in respect of a prosecution of one Michael Paul Falzon.'

On the same day, five charges against Michael Paul Falzon, some relating to the offence with which Marlin was charged and some relating to the cultivation of cannabis, were listed to be heard.

I and Falzon's lawyer objected to the charges being heard together. In response to the objection the Crown Prosecutor, a Mr Callinan, said:

There is something of an irregularity in that these matters are not joined on the one Bench Charge Sheet. That's a matter that can be easily remedied, it's simply a matter of ... a mechanical matter of reducing the separate charges onto one Bench Charge Sheet, that's not the real issue in my submission. That's expected obviously on one of a number of grounds, one of which is that the defendant, Falzon, was arrested sometime after the arrest of the defendant Marlin. All that could have been done by the Prosecution to bring these matters before the one Court making it obvious to all parties that it was proposed by the Prosecution to proceed on all matters, has been done, again with the exception of the cigarette matter, if I can call it that, it was always indicated that ... there would be no attempt to have that heard jointly with the others.

Notwithstanding that concession was to the 'irregularity', the magistrate was inclined to proceed, and he did so over the next few days: 26–30 September 1988, 24–25 October 1988 and 21 November 1988.

On 31 January 1989, an indictment was presented in the Mackay Supreme Court charging seven separate accounts of offending by Michael Paul Falzon and Marlin.

On 16 October 1989, Mr Tony Glynn presented an indictment in the District Court at Townsville, charging Brian Rodney Marlin with two separate counts: first a charge of demanding property with threats and secondly, a count of non-judicial official corruption.

The full text of the charges was as follows:

That on a date unknown between the 22nd day of January 1987 and the 11th day of April 1987 at Mackay, in the State of Queensland, you orally demanded from one Gerard John Falzon[1] without a reasonable or probable cause a sum of money namely $2000 with a threat that the said Gerard John Falzon would be charged with an offence if the said Gerard John Falzon did not comply with the said demand and with the intent thereby to extort money from the said Gerard John Falzon.

And further that on a date unknown between the 22nd day of January 1987 and the 11th day of April 1987 at Mackay, in the State of Queensland, and you being a person employed in the public service in a nonjudicial capacity, namely as a Police Officer in which capacity you were concerned in the prosecution of offenders, corruptly received from Gerard John Falzon a sum of money namely $2000 on account of you committing the charge of the said Gerard John Falzon with an offence with a view to the protection of an offender from punishment.

Marlin pleaded not guilty to both counts.

The trial continued over 10 days.

On day eight, a significant dispute arose about what questions might be asked by me concerning the investigation into any receiving or other possible charges against Gerard Falzon in respect to the possession of cigarettes that may or may not have been stolen was

---

1   Gerard John Falzon owned Paradise Nights Nightclub.

irrelevant and so he was not going to allow me to proceed to ask questions about that.

After lunch on that day, I asked His Honour to reserve for the consideration of the Full Court a question of law arising from that ruling. His Honour enquired of me, 'Is it mandatory?'

I replied, 'Yes.'

As it turned out, this was a significant turning point in the trial because it seemed to me that His Honour was not anxious to state the case for the consideration of the Court of Criminal Appeal.

On day nine at the end of the day, the trial Judge was indicating some doubt about the sufficiency of the evidence.

Before adjourning on the ninth day the trial judge said:

> Let me just read this passage to you and it is one that has been adopted by the Court in Sutton's case, paragraph 2; "The difficulty arises where there is some evidence but it is ... inconsistent with other evidence and then the Judge has a duty to stop it." I find in this case so far on the evidence that the case depends upon the evidence of Gerard Falzon. There are serious inconsistencies within his evidence – and I have been through the transcript and noted all of those – some significant inconsistencies. There is also evidence which is inconsistent with his version and it seems to me that the case falls within those words. When you have a case which required corroboration, if you can get it, before it falls into that category of being dangerous – where you are left with a main witness upon whom we have to rely beyond reasonable doubt before there can be a conviction – and then there are those inconsistencies – I have been through this passage at page 135 of his evidence – I just don't see in the evidence, having regard now to the

> *evidence of Mr Henkel, how any jury could convict properly. I don't know – I will consider it overnight, but having been through it that is my feeling at present.*

After some further argument, the court was adjourned until the following day.

On day 10, some further witnesses were called before lunch and then I made a submission that the case should not be left to the jury. His Honour considered the matter over the lunch break and when we resumed after lunch he said:

> *At the close of the case for the Crown, submissions were made that I should take the case from the Jury, that is, I should direct a verdict of not guilty. Just briefly, to outline a few things, the accused has entered a plea of not guilty. He has been interviewed a number of times and at a lengthy record of interview maintained his innocence. His superior officer, a Mr Bruton, described him as an excellent detective, good, reliable and honest. That police officer has not in any way been tainted by the Fitzgerald Inquiry and seems to have been promoted to bigger and better things.*
>
> *Now, the evidence against the accused relies upon Gerard Falzon. He gave evidence that he had given $2000 to the accused because of a threat by the accused that Falzon would suffer some detriment if that didn't happen. Apart from the evidence of Falzon there is some evidence which is consistent with the allegation of Gerard Falzon. This is in relation to the notebooks and a file which is missing, but in my view, although consistent, it is not in this case capable of being corroboration.*
>
> *We go further then to examine the position so far as Gerard Falzon is concerned. He has been given an indemnity in relation to this matter and will not be prosecuted provided he abides by the terms of that indemnity. That is a factor*

to be born in mind, of course, the jury, if it does proceed that far, will have to be warned, having regard to the fact that he is a witness giving evidence under an indemnity.

It is clear that the charges which have been brought against the accused, if one accepts the version of Gerard Falzon, he is an accomplice and as a matter of law certain consequences follow upon that as well. When one looks at his evidence, in many aspects it has been vague. There are a number of inconsistencies within the evidence. These inconsistencies are not minor. They clearly are major matters so far as his evidence is concerned. I will not detail all of these at this stage, but they are matters upon which he could not be mistaken and in my view, they are serious reflections on his credit. For example, there is the suggestion that he visited the police station shortly after Detective Marlin commenced this investigation. If one examined his evidence on another occasion and before, clearly, one would have formed the impression that this was not so.

After he was made aware of the statement by a particular Constable - Constable Henkel I think it was – he came to the view that it was possible. In this Courtroom to examine his evidence on this point we find it very difficult to follow, but he accepted that he may have been interviewed by Detective Marlin at the police station in connection with the cigarettes. If one accepts the evidence of the Constable Henkel again, that is a very serious reflection upon the reliability of Gerard Falzon.

In addition to that, there is, as I say, not only inconsistencies in his evidence, there is a body of evidence which is inconsistent with the evidence of Gerard Falzon. I refer first of all to the evidence on Constable Henkel. There is also the evidence of Sam Falzon, his brother. Sam Falzon disagrees on an important matter as to where the cigarettes came *from and as to the knowledge on the part of Gerard Falzon when they came into the possession of Gerard Falzon.*

I have no doubt that pressure was put on Sam Falzon at some stage by Gerard Falzon to have Sam Falzon change his version of the event which he was giving to the police. An extraordinary incident occurred in the motel room in Mackay where Sam Falzon was being interviewed by the police. He initially gave one version, the police left the room, after the matter was discussed by Sam Falzon, Gerard Falzon and their solicitor, Mr Iain Duncan, when the police returned Sam Falzon's version was then similar or consistent with what his brother had been saying. Some two days later Sam Falzon reverted to the position which he gave in this Court room and his sworn evidence is clearly in conflict on a major point of Gerard Falzon. Sam Falzon was a credible witness. He is not under any indemnity, as far as I have ever been aware, and if one accepts the evidence of Sam Falzon, then Gerard Falzon has told lies. He has told lies on oath on several occasions.

In total then, evaluation of the evidence and the case against the accused in my view is seriously deficient. I would direct the jury that it would be dangerous to convict, that having considered all the evidence they should or ought to entertain a reasonable doubt and that any conviction which would be recorded could only be regarded as unsafe".

The Crown prosecutor sought the return of the indictment and endorsed the indictment that the Crown would not proceed further upon it.

I asked the trial judge to direct that a verdict of not guilty be entered. The Crown prosecutor said that he would not stand in the way of that. The trial Judge then said this:

I am not going to direct a verdict because having viewed all of the authorities which I find it difficult to follow in certain respects, that is the formula which I put. It comes in, of course, the formula which was used by the Court of Criminal Appeal in the Bradley case to which I have referred, but it is not directing an acquittal. It is pointing out to the jury that the evidence is as I have stated. I will explain all of these matters to the jury. I think they should understand them. The matter has been fully investigated and I like to keep juries informed as to what is happening so they understand the working of our system. Sometimes I think they wonder whether they are redundant. I certainly don't want the jury to gain that impression. I might add, Mr Glynn, that in the circumstances I think you are taking a very proper course and it is in fact most heartening to me to see a man in your position prepared to take that course and assume his responsibilities.

The jury returned and was discharged.

When Gene Paterson and I left the Courtroom with Marlin a short time later, a number of the jurors were waiting. We initially wondered why they were waiting but it became apparent that they had stayed so that they could shake hands with Brian Marlin and congratulate him on the outcome.

Never before or since have I seen such a thing happen.

Harris and Northern Sandblasting, 1995 QCA 413; 1997 188 CLR 313

Nicole Anne Harris suffered a severe electrical shock injury at a rented house where she was living with her parents and a brother on 4 June 1987. She was nine years old. What she did was turn off a tap in the garden at her mother's request. She had no way of knowing that because of the careless way in which an electrician had repaired a hotplate on the stove, the tap was carrying a high-voltage electric charge.

She survived but was left without the capacity of speech, thought or independent movement. The electrical work that caused the tap to be carrying the high voltage electric charge had been performed by the first defendant only a couple of days before the plaintiff sustained her injury.

In my experience, in many matters where severe injuries are sustained, somebody in the injured person's family steps forward and provides care and attention above and beyond what anyone could imagine. In this case, it was the plaintiff's mother who not only devoted herself full-time to caring for the injured plaintiff but organised a roster of friends, family and acquaintances who provided 24-hour care to the plaintiff.

I appeared for her at the trial before Justice Derrington in Townsville I was led by CF Wall QC.

The action was brought against Brian Briggs (the electrician who had repaired the stove), the North Queensland Electricity Board (the electricity supplier) and Northern Sandblasting Proprietary Limited (the owners of the house in question).

A judgment for a sum in excess of $1 million was entered in the plaintiff's favour against the electrician. The other defendants escaped liability.

An appeal was instituted against the dismissal of the action as far as the owner of the house was concerned.

The Queensland Court of Appeal (Appeal number 120 of 1994 – 1995 QCA 413) allowed the appeal (by a 2–1 majority), leaving an opening for the insurer to take the matter further.

Not surprisingly, an appeal was brought to the High Court. That appeal was heard and determined by seven

Justices of the High Court (1997) HCA 39. In a judgment given on 14 August 1987 (more than 10 years after the plaintiff suffered injuries), the High Court dismissed the insurer's appeal.

Sadly, from the community's point of view, several separate judgments were delivered and when I finished practising to go the District Court of Queensland in 2010, there was still argument about what the true meaning and effect of the High Court's judgment was.

The case had a sad footnote. An outpouring of community sympathy for the injured plaintiff resulted in a good deal of money being raised to assist her. Her father absconded with a good deal of the money and was not brought back to Queensland for several years. When he was brought back, he was convicted and punished for that offence.

When the plaintiff died in her teenage years there was still a significant amount of the money remaining and because she did not have the capacity to make a will and did not have any other dependents. Her parents shared equally in what remained of the damages.

A legal outcome but not a good one.

Valleyfied Pty Ltd v Primac Ltd And Anor[1]

This case was one of my most unsatisfactory experiences at the Queensland Bar. Shortly after my appointment as Senior Counsel, I was approached by a Townsville solicitor to see whether I would accept a brief concerning the failure of a watering system installed by Netafim at the request of Primac on two farms owned by the plaintiff in the Burdekin.

The case was very interesting and my junior and I spent many, many hours in research and preparation for a trial which took some time to complete. Those who wish

---

1   2002 QSC 134 – Cullinane, J.

to read all the gory details will see that I have included the reference to the trial Judge's judgment and the Court of Appeal decision in a footnote. Perusal of those judgments will show that the initial trial commenced on 18 February 2002 and continued until 8 March 2002. The appeal was heard on 24, 25 and 26 February 2003, but the decision was not given until 8 August 2003.

My point is this – the trial judge's decision was an impeccable one. The Court of Appeal, by majority, decided that the trial judge had not made a sufficient discount for continencies (which he plainly had). That resulted in the Court of Appeal wrongly reducing the damages very substantially.

More importantly, from my point of view, it resulted in all the Townsville lawyers being sacked by the principal of the plaintiff company, who somehow managed to escape without paying a penny for the services received up until the end of the Court of Appeal decision. That occurred because its governing director was well known to, and trusted by, my instructing solicitor, who was devastated when he and the company refused to pay.

The director retained Gold Coast solicitors who picked up the easiest Special Leave Application imaginable. That the trial judge was correct about discounting[1] and that the Court of Appeal got it completely wrong[2] was obvious on a cursory reading of the respective judgments.

Considering that the Court of Appeal decision was not given until more than five months after the argument was heard, it was both surprising and disappointing, to me at least, that more time had not been spent reading the judgment under appeal.

A very unusual outcome occurred in the High Court of Australia. That court ordered that the Special Leave Application (special leave being necessary to appeal

---

1 See para 97 of the trial judge's judgement.
2 See para 45 of the Court of Appeal decision.

against a decision of this nature) should be treated as the hearing of the appeal, that the appeal should be allowed and the decision of the trial judge reinstated.

I have not studied the statistics of High Court Special Leave Applications, but I am told that you could count on the fingers of one hand the number of times such a thing has occurred.

Sadly, while we could draw some intellectual satisfaction from the fact that matters were put right so readily, it did not assist those who did the real work in obtaining any reward for their efforts. What it did do for me was leave me extremely wary of allowing any matter in which I was involved to finish up in the tender care of the Court of Appeal.

The Queen and Smith[3]

Philip Gerard Smith was engaged in an altercation at the Bank Nightclub in Townsville on 20 May 2005. A young man died as a result.

Smith was tried in Townsville by Judge and jury. I appeared on his behalf.

The judge was about to retire and was enjoying a tour of the state before doing so. It was difficult to get him to focus on anything but his next social engagement as the trial progressed.

The Crown prosecutor behaved very badly. He called several witnesses who knew the accused and were engaged in similar nightclub occupations. All of them gave evidence that was at least capable of supporting the accused man's defence. When the time came for addresses to be made to the jury, the Crown prosecutor attacked them all, suggesting that they had conspired together to defeat the Crown. No suggestion of that type had ever been made to any of the witnesses.

---

3   2007 QCA 447.

The accused was convicted and sentenced to six years imprisonment on 29 June 2007 (a little more than two years after the incident occurred). His appeal was heard five months later in the Court of Criminal Appeal and judgment was given on 19 December 2007 (two and half years after the incident).

The Court of Appeal allowed his appeal, set aside his conviction and ordered a retrial.

The following is taken from the judgment of the President of the Court of Appeal:

> *(49). The Prosecutor did not continue with any inflammatory aspects of his address after Defence Counsel unsuccessfully applied for a mistrial. But nothing he said to the jury subsequently was in any way adequate to undo the harmful comments previously made. The Judge, either when the jury returned to listen to the remainder of the Prosecutor's address or in his later summing up to the jury, did nothing to pour water on the wildfire ignited by the Prosecutor. Understandably, Defence Counsel in his address had to return to the Prosecutor's inflammatory statements and attempt to meet them. But it was not Defence Counsel's task to set up the framework for a fair trial for his client. The appellant was entitled to a fairly conducted prosecution.*

The following is taken from the judgement of Justice Keane:

> *(57). It may be that the unfairness which thus arose did not necessitate the discharge of the jury, in that it could have been remedied by a sufficiently strong direction from the trial Judge to the jury to disregard this aspect of the Crown Prosecutor's address. Unfortunately, no direction in any way apt to defuse this unfair argument was given by the trial Judge to the jury.*

Rough justice?

Fingleton and the Queen[1]

Diane Fingleton was the Chief Magistrate of the Magistrate's Court of Queensland. She was convicted of an offence against the criminal code in connection with some instructions she had given to another Magistrate. Not only was she convicted, but she was sentenced to actual imprisonment and spent time in prison, which must have been an ordeal for someone who had occupied the position that she'd had.

Her appeal was dealt with by the Queensland Court of Appeal[2] and dismissed. She appealed to the High Court of Australia. The High Court of Australia allowed her appeal and set aside conviction and sentence[3] based on a provision in the Magistrates Court Act of Queensland, which gave her protection in respect of any such decision. How it could be that this section was not raised and relied upon in her initial trial in the District Court of Queensland or the Court of Appeal beggars belief.

I once heard a senior member of the Queensland judiciary say that everyone who had been involved in the case knew of the section but did not think it had application. It is very difficult to accept that as an explanation because, as one who spent many years defending people in criminal Courts, I know that one did not have to be persuaded that an argument would necessarily be successful before deciding to raise it where a penalty of the extreme sort imposed upon Diane Fingleton might result at trial.

Another version of events is that the relevant section became known to the Queenslanders involved in the case when one of the High Court Justices sent his associate to deliver a message to all counsel involved, telling

---

1   2003 QCA 266.
2   2003 QCA 266.
3   2005 227 CLR 166.

them that he would like to hear submissions about the particular section when the appeal came on for hearing.

Whatever the true explanation, the whole thing was a sad day for Queensland justice.

Cardinal George Pell

In my opinion, the greatest injustice of all during my legal lifetime occurred in respect of Cardinal George Pell.

I am not by any means a supporter of Cardinal Pell, but I am a believer that justice must be done by a criminal law system that involves proper careful investigation by police and proper careful consideration by prosecutors before a man is put on trial. It seems to me that neither of those things occurred in the case of Cardinal Pell.

Background

Timeline of Cardinal Pell's career:

- 8 June 1941 – George Pell was born in Ballarat, the son of a gold miner and an Irish Catholic. He was raised in a Ballarat home that had been built by his maternal grandfather.
- 1966 – ordained a Priest for the Ballarat diocese in St Peter's Basilica.
- 1971 – appointed assistant Priest at Swan Hill.
- 1973–1983 – assistant Priest at the Ballarat East Parish.
- 1978–1979 – Episcopal Vicar for Education in the Ballarat diocese.
- 1987 – appointed Auxiliary Bishop of Melbourne.
- 1983 – Pell accompanies priest Gerard Ridsdale to Court in Melbourne. Ridsdale was later convicted of a string of serious child sex abuse charges

and became known as one of Australia's most notorious paedophile priests.

- 1996 – appointed Archbishop of Melbourne
- 2001 – appointed Archbishop of Sydney, the Australian Catholic Church's most senior position.
- 2003 – appointed to the Sacred College of Cardinals by Pope John Paul II.
- 2014 – appointed to be the first Prefect of the Church's Secretariat for the Economy – in effect the Vatican's Treasurer. He is welcomed into the Pope's inner circle of trusted advisors known as the Group of Nine or C9.

The Investigation

- 2015 – a man in his 30s contacted police to report that he was sexually abused by Pell in the 1990s as a choirboy at St Patrick's Cathedral. He also reported that his friend, who died in accidental circumstances as an adult, was also sexually assaulted by Pell.
- 20 February 2016 – it was revealed that a Victorian police task force had been investigating historical sexual abuse allegations against Cardinal Pell.
- 28 February 2016 – giving evidence from Rome to the Royal Commission into Institutional Responses to Child Sexual Abuse in Australia, Cardinal Pell admits to 'catastrophic failures' by the Catholic church in relation to child sex abuse, an issue he says was on his radar from the 1970s.
- 27 July 27 2016 – the ABC's *7.30 Report* details complaints about Cardinal Pell, which were being investigated by the Victorian police.

- October 2016 – Victorian detectives travel to Rome to meet Cardinal Pell, who voluntarily participates in an interview. He emphatically denies the allegations when they are put to him.

- February 2017 – a police brief of evidence regarding sex assault allegations against Cardinal Pell is handed to prosecutors for review.

- 13 May 2017 – ABC journalist Louise Milligan's book Cardinal: *The Rise And Fall of George Pell* is published. The book contains new allegations of sexual abuse against Cardinal Pell.

- 14 May 2017 – Cardinal Pell's lawyers strongly deny the allegations raised in the book.

- 16 May 2017 – Victorian police receive advice from the Director of Public Prosecutions about the Brief of Evidence. Police refuse to comment.

- 18 May 2017 – Cardinal Pell restates his innocence in Rome, saying, 'We have to respect due process, wait until it is concluded and, obviously, I will continue to cooperate fully.'

- 25 May 2017 – Victorian Police Chief Commissioner Graham Ashton says a decision about charging Cardinal Pell is 'imminent'.

- 29 June 2017 – Victorian police announce that Cardinal Pell will be charged on summons in relation to 'multiple' offences. In Rome, Cardinal Pell denies the allegations and says, 'I'm looking forward, finally, to have my day in court.' He returns to Australia in the following days.

- 26 July 2017 – Cardinal Pell faces Melbourne Magistrates Court, where his lawyer Robert Richter QC, says his client intends to plead not guilty to the charges.

- 1 March 2018 – prosecutors announce they will withdraw one of the charges because one of the accusers has died.

- 5 March 2018 – Pell faces Melbourne Magistrates Court for a committal hearing, which determines whether he is to face trial.

- 1 May 2018 – Magistrate Belinda Wellington commits Pell to stand trial on multiple charges of historical sexual assault involving multiple accusers. She strikes out some of the charges. Pell pleads not guilty.

- 15 August 2018 – Pell's first trial starts in the County Court on allegations he sexually abused two 13-year-old choir boys in the 1990s when he was Archbishop of Melbourne. Pell pleads not guilty to five charges.

- 20 September 2018 – the jury is discharged after it is unable to reach a verdict after five days of deliberations.

- 7 November 2018 – a retrial begins on the same allegations. Pell pleads not guilty to five charges.

- 11 December 2018 – Pell is found guilty of five charges of sexual assault. Chief Judge Peter Kidd grants bail for Pell to return to court in February 2019 for the presentence hearing but advises him he will be remanded in custody after the hearing. The verdict cannot be reported due to a Suppression Order put in place and ahead of another trial Pell is due to face over allegations he abused boys at a swimming pool in Ballarat in the 1970s. Pell is allowed to travel to Sydney on bail for knee surgery.

- 26 February 2019 – Pell's guilty verdict is revealed publicly for the first time after the other swimming pool trial is abandoned due to lack of admissible evidence and the Suppression Order is lifted.

- 27 February 2019 – Pell returns to court for a presentence hearing and is remanded in custody. His legal team launches an appeal.

- 13 March 2019 – Pell is sentenced to six years jail, with a non-parole period of three years and eight months. He signs the sex offenders' register.

- 5–6 June 2019 – Pell returns to court for an appeal hearing, where his lawyers argue why he should be acquitted.

- 21 August 2019 – the Victorian Court of Appeal Judges reject Pell's appeal by a 2–1 majority and the convictions for historic child sex abuse are upheld.

- 17 September 2019 – Cardinal Pell's lawyers take his fight to the High Court.

- 13 November 2019 – the High Court refers Pell's application for special leave to appeal to the Full Bench of the High Court.

- 11 March 2020 – Pell's appeal is heard by the Full Bench of the High Court.

- 7 April 2020 – the High Court unanimously allows Cardinal Pell's appeal, finding the jury should have entertained a doubt over his guilt.

- 7 May 2020 – Unredacted sections of the Child Abuse Royal Commission findings are released revealing Cardinal Pell was 'conscious of child sexual abuse by clergy' as early as 1973 and failed to act on complaints about priests.

Legal Background

It used to be the case that in any offence of a sexual nature, there were special rules to be applied.

First, a person could not be convicted in the absence of evidence that amounted to corroboration. Corroboration was defined. Corroboration meant evidence independent of the complaining party which did two things – first, tended to confirm that the offence was committed and second, tended to confirm that it was the defendant who committed the offence.

For example, the very best form of corroboration was an admission or confession by the defendant.

Other examples of corroboration would be injury consistent with the complaint (to prove the commission of the offence) and some additional evidence placing the defendant with the complaining party at the relevant time, or injury to the defendant consistent with the nature of the complaint being made.

Time will not permit an exhaustive examination of all forms of evidence that might constitute corroboration today, but it is important to understand this is part of the background of the modern method of prosecuting sexual offences.

The second important matter to remember is what is called recent complaint.

When I was training to be a lawyer, the absence of recent complaint was a significant thing that was thought to tell against the credibility of a person complaining.

Both of those things were critically important to anyone charged with the responsibility of defending a person accused of a sexual offence. Prosecuting authorities would often elect not to prosecute because of the absence of one or the other of those things. Prosecutions often failed because of the failure to prove one or the other of those things.

With the passage of time, it came to be thought that these rules were unfair to the complaining party and so the law was amended to do away with the requirement for corroboration and to prohibit comment being made in the absence of a recent complaint. This meant that a person accused could be convicted on the word of his accuser without any supporting material.

As you can imagine, court lists became crowded with what are called 'word against word' prosecutions.

The accused person often faced particular difficulty because in the case of a historical complaint, while the complainer can often give a detailed, factual description of what he or she asserts was done 15, 20 or 25 years ago, the accused person can often not do more than make a general denial as so many people cannot account for their movements in any detail after such a long period of time.

The task of a tribunal of fact, most often a jury, is therefore extremely difficult. They are invited to consider whether they thought the complaining party a credible and honest person and if they did, then notwithstanding the accused person's sworn denial and the absence of any supporting material, to convict.

Lots of people have complaints about their experiences in courts, saying that they were wrongly convicted of speeding or some other offence. A wrongful conviction for a sexual offence, particularly against a child, is in a quite different category, not just because of the reputational damage that is done but because prison is mandatory and it is, I think, well understood that persons convicted of such offending do not have an easy time in prison.

My own experience in the time that I was a judge was that juries often struggled to complete the task. That was, I think, at least in part because of the very emotionally charged atmosphere that often surrounds such trials.

In recent years, there has been much publicity about sexual offending, which leaves people thinking that anyone alleging sexual offending is probably telling the truth.

A recent example can be found in the writing of Louise Milligan, an author and investigative reporter for ABC television's *Four Corners* program. The updated edition of her book *The Rise and Fall of George Pell* went on sale in late March 2019.[1] She claims to have kept an open mind about Pell's guilt, but if what is published in the April edition of the *Australian Women's Weekly* is an accurate representation of the book, I find it a little difficult to believe that she is an impartial observer.

She claims to have learned by researching Royal Commission Archives '... that it takes an average of 25.7 years for survivors of child sexual abuse to come forward'. I do not think that any reasonable person would readily accept such a claim without knowing more.

Statistics is, after all, a subject that involves evaluation not just calculation. As Mark Twain once said, 'There are lies, there are damn lies and there are statistics.'

Having said that, I must acknowledge that Louise Milligan was awarded an Australian Press Council Press Freedom Medal for her reporting on the George Pell investigation and conviction. She is a Melbourne-based investigative reporter for *Four Corners* and the *7.30 Report*.

As I said earlier, I am not and never have been a fan of Cardinal Pell. His efforts with the Melbourne Response to Child Sexual Abuse (a controversial scheme that meant that victims initially received no more than $50,000 each, later increased to $75,000 then $150,000

---

1   Milligan's book was published in May 2017, withdrawn from sale, but returned in March 2019.

each) resulted in the Catholic Church avoiding payments in excess of $50 million to sexual abuse victims.

He also played a significant part in the establishment and maintenance of what became known as the 'Ellis Defence'. That defence was named after John Ellis, a former altar boy who tried to sue the Church for abuse he had suffered at the hands of a Priest. As his abuser had died and the Church had been structured as an unincorporated association – a body that barely exists in legal terms – Ellis was left with no one to sue.

Under the Ellis Defence, the Catholic Church's wealth in Australia (estimated in 2017 to be in the order of $76.5 billion worth of property and other assets with an annual income of $11.5 million a year from businesses in the areas of education, health and welfare services) was out of reach of victims in pursuit of compensation.

This contrasted with the situation in America, where billions were awarded against the Church for similar crimes. The largest single settlement in the USA was against the Archdioceses of Los Angeles, which in 2007 paid out $660 million to 508 victims of clerical abuse.

Although the Church's own investigation found that it was likely that Ellis had been abused, rather than offering him an apology or compensation, the Church, under Pell's direction, spent $1.5 million on a legal assault. When Ellis lost his case on appeal, the Church pursued him for costs at Pell's direction.

Another interesting event involving Cardinal Pell concerned a person named Julie Stewart, who complained of having been abused by a Father Peter Searson (described by Louise Milligan in her book as a Brycreamed paedophile Priest who carried a gun around the parish school at Doveton).

Years later, when giving evidence to the Victorian Parliamentary Enquiry into Child Abuse, Cardinal Pell denied knowing anything about sexual abuse at Doveton, saying only, 'There might be victims'

It was also necessary, I think, to bear in mind the relationship that Pell maintained with Father Ridsdale, a notorious sex offender who abused a great number of children and was moved from diocese to diocese to keep a lid on the complaints. Cardinal Pell said more than once that he was not aware that Father Ridsdale was a sex offender. If he did not know, then he was probably one of the very small number of people who did not know about Ridsdale's wrongdoing. It is extremely difficult to accept his assertion about this because he was at times remarkably close to Ridsdale, even supporting him through Court proceedings.

So it will hardly come as a surprise that a person like me, who devoted much of his life to acting on behalf of injured people, had no admiration for Pell's efforts to preserve the Church's assets against claims that were known to be meritorious.

Nonetheless, if we are to have a legal system that is worth having, we must make sure that everybody gets a fair trial. Had Pell been convicted of some offence relating to covering up the activities of paedophile Priests, failing to act appropriately to protect children from the activities of paedophile Priests, or even to giving false evidence about his knowledge of their activities, I would have had no sympathy for him at all. Having said that, there are significant issues surrounding the offences for which he was convicted and which attracted intense press coverage such that his life will be forever damaged.

There is, it seems to me, a significant difference between being a person who failed to act appropriately in the face of evidence of paedophilia and a person who was a perpetrator of paedophilia. My views on this topic are probably influenced by the fact that I grew up in an era where a person could not be convicted of a sexual offence unless there was corroboration.

As happened in Pell's case, the jury was invited to consider whether or not the complainant was a convincing believable witness, and if they thought he was, to proceed to conviction notwithstanding all the evidence that tended to disprove the truth of the allegations.

In the case of Pell, we know that:

- He was convicted of the five charges on the word of the sole surviving choirboy who gave evidence that he was molested in 1996 and 1997 and that a fellow choirboy was molested by Pell in 1996

- There was no evidence of a forensic nature

- There was no evidence of a pattern of behaviour

- There was no confession (indeed there was a comprehensive interview with police officers in which Pell made robust denials)

- The sacristy in which the offending was alleged to have occurred was an almost public area to which a door or doors were open at all times

- The boys were not known to Pell and he was not known to them prior to the offending so the usual grooming was not found

- By the time Pell was brought to trial one of the boys was deceased, but it was known that he had been asked about the event and had said that nothing of the sort described by the surviving boy had in fact occurred

- The choirboy who gave evidence said that two choirboys had left the liturgical procession and gone to the sacristy where they began drinking the church wine. He said Pell arrived suddenly, censured them and then with the sacristy door open and people passing by in the corridor and still in his heavy mass vestments including the alb, proceeded to sexually assault the boys, whom he did not know, in an extremely brief period of time.

- The Crown prosecutor asked the jury, 'Did he strike you as an honest witness?'
- It must be remembered that the test in such a trial is proof 'beyond reasonable doubt'. How satisfactory is it that a jury should be invited to weigh apparently implausible evidence against the apparent credibility of the complainant? Is that a satisfactory way to reach a conclusion that is said to be a conclusion beyond reasonable doubt?[1]

The Appeal Court was faced with a difficult decision having regard to the intense media pressure and the generally delighted reaction of our nation's press and politicians to the fall from grace of one of the Church's leaders.

This highlights a problem generally found with 'historical' sexual cases. Anyone with experience in the practice of criminal law, particularly since the introduction of the amendments that mean that no corroboration is required, will be aware that there are sometimes truthful witnesses who are most unimpressive witnesses and untruthful witnesses who are sometimes very impressive witnesses.

Public confidence in legal proceedings will be maintained only where the public can be confident that convictions only result in cases where there has been a proper detailed and impartial consideration of *all* the evidence.

No thinking person could imagine that Pell is a nice man.

No thinking person could imagine that he had not been subject to trial by media before any hearing began.

---

1   2019 VCC 260.

No thinking person could imagine that where 376 companies and individuals remain to be dealt with for breach of Suppression Orders made after the first trial (where no result could be reached), can it confidently be said that Pell received a fair trial.

The Trial Judge

His Honour, Chief Judge Peter Kidd, was appointed to the Country Court of Victoria on 5 October 2015. He is a graduate of the University of Adelaide and prior to his appointment, was a very experienced prosecutor. He came to the Bar in Victoria in 1995 and prosecuted such well-known cases as the conspiracy allegations against Bruno Grollo and others, and the case arising from the abduction, rape and murder of a Bega schoolgirl, as well as the very known and high-profile prosecution of the murders of police Sergeant Gary Silk and Senior Constable Rodney Miller.

I would ask:

- Is there a strong case for trial by judge alone when a high-profile figure is charged with the sort of offences that Pell was charged with?

- Where a case depends upon the unsupported word of a complainant, is it not incumbent upon the prosecuting authority to exercise a discretion not to proceed where there is not only no corroborative evidence but all the available evidence from other sources is inconsistent with that of the complainant?

- Is there not a good case for restoring the trial Judge's discretion to stop a prosecution at the conclusion of the Crown case where the evidence is as unsatisfactory, as it was in Pell's case?

In several American states time limits have been legislated with respect not only to sexual offences but to all kinds of criminal offences save those that carry very heavy penalties. This is one way of dealing with the problem. Another would be to reintroduce the requirement for corroboration, if not generally, then at least in the case of historical sex offences.

I remember thinking on more than one occasion, when I was presiding at a trial of a historical sexual offence, how fortunate I was to be able to leave the decision-making to a jury as it seemed to me that so often it came down to a matter of guesswork. Is that not a most unsatisfactory outcome for the complainant? Would it not have been better to let the person pursue a civil claim and leave it at that?

It is necessary to understand the nature of the allegations made before continuing this discussion about the appeal, particularly in respect of the 'impossibility' ground. I have taken this summary from paragraphs 43–50 of the Court of Appeal decision (the majority decision).

Before proceeding with the details of the complaints it is necessary to understand that:

1. In what follows, it was the surviving chorister who gave evidence

2. The chorister who died in 2014 had never complained

The First Incident (Charges 1–4):

The prosecution case was that after Sunday solemn mass in the latter part of 1996, Cardinal Pell committed a number of sexual offences against two choristers who were then 13 years old. The prosecution relied upon the evidence of 'A', namely, that he and his friend 'B' had detached themselves from the choir during its procession out of the cathedral. A said that they re-entered the cathedral via the south transept. The two then made their way along the sacristy corridor. They entered the priest's sacristy, an area that was off-limits to choristers.

A had no recollection of ever being in this room before. Evidence was given by Charles Porelli that, during the latter part of 1996, the Priest's sacristy was being used by the Archbishop for robing and disrobing due to the unavailability of the Archbishop's sacristy.

It is interesting to note that in a footnote to this paragraph, the majority said:

> *It may not be entirely correct to say that 'A's evidence was uncorroborated. To an extent his evidence was supported by reference to knowledge that he possessed which he could not have come by unless he was telling the truth. In any event, there is nothing particularly unusual in a jury convicting an accused on the strength of a so-called 'uncorroborated' complainant. A finding of guilt in such circumstances does not give rise, in and of itself to a conviction being unsafe or unsatisfactory.*

Once inside the Priest's sacristy, A and B made their way to an alcove in the corner (described as a wood-panelled area resembling a storage kitchenette with cupboards), which was a little bit concealed. There they located some sacramental wine. This was from the panelled area in the cupboards. As they began 'swigging' the wine, they had barely opened the bottle and taken a couple of swigs when Cardinal Pell entered the room alone. He was wearing robes. Cardinal Pell planted himself in the doorway and said something like, 'What are you doing here?' or 'You're in trouble.' The boys froze and then Cardinal Pell undid his trousers or belt. He started moving underneath his robes.

B was saying, 'Can you let us go? We didn't do anything.' After pulling B aside, Cardinal Pell pulled out his penis and grabbed B's head. A could see Cardinal Pell's hands around the back of B's head. B was crouched before Cardinal Pell and his legs were flailing around a bit. B's head was being controlled and it was down near Cardinal Pell's genitals. 'A' heard some whimpering and heard B's discomfort. He saw that B's face looked terrified. This took place for barely a minute or two (charge 1).

Then Cardinal Pell turned to A and pushed his penis into A's mouth. A was pushed down and crouching or kneeling closer to the corner of the room where the cupboards were. Cardinal Pell was standing. His penis was erect. A was 'freaking out'. This happened for a period of time. It would not have been any more than two minutes (charge 2).

Cardinal Pell then instructed A to undo his pants and take them off. A dropped his pants and underwear. Cardinal Pell started touching A's penis and testicles with his hands (charge 3). As he did this, Cardinal Pell was using his other hand to touch his own penis (charge 4). Cardinal Pell was sort of crouched almost on one knee. The two instances of touching took a minute or two.

The two boys made some objections but did not quite yell. They were sobbing, in shock and whimpering. During the offending, Cardinal Pell told them to be quiet, trying to stop them from crying.

After Cardinal Pell had stopped, A gathered himself and his clothing. He and B exited the cathedral the same way as they had entered, via the sacristy corridor to the south transept. They entered the choir room very quickly after what had happened and re-joined some of the choir who were mingling around and finishing up for the day. The two then left the Cathedral precinct. A did not complain to anyone, including his parents on the ride home or at any time after. Nor did he ever discuss the offending with B.

The Second Incident (Charge 5)

At least a month after the first incident, again following a Sunday solemn mass at St Patrick's Cathedral, A was proceeding with the choir back through the sacristy corridor towards the choir room. As A was walking between the entry to the Priest's sacristy and the Archbishop's sacristy, Cardinal Pell pushed himself up against A and squeezed A's testicles and penis over his robes. Cardinal Pell was robed at the time. He did not say anything. A did not tell B about the second incident.

A made a complaint to police in June 2015. B died in 2014, having never made any complaint to police. When asked by his mother in 2001, at age 17 or 18, whether he had ever been 'interfered with or touched up' when he was in the choir, B said, 'No.'

The Victorian Court of Criminal Appeal

Pell's appeal was heard in the Court of Appeal in Victoria (presiding Chief Anne Ferguson, President of the Court of Appeal, Justice Chris Maxwell and Justice Mark Weinberg) on 5 and 6 June 2019.

On 21 August 2019, a decision was given.[1]

The judgment comprises a total of about 300 pages – approximately 100 written by the majority (Ferguson and Maxwell JJ) and approximately 200 written by Weinberg J. It is not a straightforward document for a lawyer to comprehend, let alone a layman. However, the following might be said about it.

The majority generally followed the line adopted by the prosecution at trial, saying that if the complainant's evidence was judged to be credible and compelling then there was nothing in the independent evidence which compelled a finding in Pell's favour.

Weinberg J, on the other hand, took a more analytical approach to **all the evidence** in the way that lawyers traditionally assess such things.

Two days after the decision was given, on Friday 23 August 2019, *The Australian* newspaper reported the

---

[1]   2019 VSCA 186.

head of the Victorian Bar as saying that, 'Dissenting Court of Appeal judgments often became roadmaps for High Court applications.' The President of the Victorian Bar Association, Matt Collins QC said, 'It is difficult to predict which cases the High Court granted leave, with the Court typically approving just 15 per cent of applications.'

He felt that Justice Weinberg's view that there were 'too many discrepancies and uncertainties to put to one side' was a major area for Pell's legal team to be examining.

On the same day, *The Australian* published an article by Tessa Akerman and John Ferguson titled 'George Pell's 'road map' to High Court' saying,

> ... unless the version of events given by the complainant is preposterous, riddled with anomalies, unless they appeared evasive or overtly dishonest, then it's a big ask to expect a (group of judges) would have a better assessment than the jury.

By the following day (24 August 2019), *The Weekend Australian* ran a headline 'The Staggering Fall of Pell' by John Ferguson. The article included the following:

> 'Nothing about this case has been simple. Despite the jury's view that the choirboy was telling the truth, one member of the Court of Appeal has matched the concerns of many others that much of what the jury found didn't necessarily add up'.

(And not just any judge but Justice Mark Weinberg, the most qualified criminal practitioner of the three of the Court of Appeal judges, cast doubt about the complainant's account).

A leading silk was reported as saying before the judgment was given that Weinberg 'will be the key'. He is the expert, and you would expect others to defer to him.

They did not.

By 27 August 2019, the same newspaper was suggesting the possibility of the Vatican running a full canonical trial into the cardinal, which could include the complainant giving evidence.

For many, the matter will never be finished.

Whatever the outcome, it is my clear opinion that the time has come to look at the way in which historical sexual complaints are dealt with.

It is one thing to say that corroboration is not required but quite another thing to say that a complainant's evidence is elevated to a special status and can be accepted notwithstanding the complete lack of support for it by other evidence.

The Victorian Court of Appeal rejected Pell's appeal by a majority of two to one. This was a surprise to me, as having watched much of the appeal, which was live-streamed, it seemed to me to be likely that the court would allow the appeal.

The judgment comprises no less than 1180 paragraphs. It is not sensible in the time allotted to me to try to give you an account of all of the arguments that were advanced and considered. I provide the reference so that anyone who wishes to can read the entire judgment and I am not sure that laymen would, in general terms, find themselves better informed by doing so.

I think that to an experienced criminal lawyer, the reasoning of Justice Weinberg (in the minority) was much more persuasive than was that of the majority (Ferguson CJ and Maxwell P).

The majority said:

351. Nothing in the tables of evidence which we have analysed in this part of our reasons leads us to the conclusion that the jury must have had a doubt about whether there was a realistic opportunity for the offending to occur, nor a doubt that the particular sexual conduct occurred. That is so whether each table is considered in isolation or in the context of the other evidence. Taking the evidence as a whole it was open to the jury to be satisfied of Cardinal Pell's guilt beyond reasonable doubt.

Justice Weinberg said:

954. Each side presented its closing submissions to the jury in a forceful, but somewhat extravagant, manner. The prosecution argued that the complainant's evidence was so obviously truthful, and reliable so compelling, that no matter what the rest of the evidence led in the trial might suggest, there could be no reasonable doubt as to the applicant's guilt. The defence argued that the complainant's account was by no means as compelling as the prosecution submitted. In any event, however, the whole of the evidence led at trial meant that the complainant's account could not be accepted. His detailed description of events, whichever version of it one considered, was 'impossible', at least realistically speaking. Self-evidently, that had to equate to a reasonable doubt.

955. Mr. Richer's submission that the complainant's account was 'impossible' was pitched at that level for effect, so far as the jury were concerned. However, there was a risk that it set a forensic hurdle that the defence never actually had to overcome. The prosecution had to establish guilt beyond reasonable doubt. The onus in that regard never shifted. Something considerably less than 'impossibility' was clearly sufficient to create such a doubt.

1100. It must be remembered, however, that the complainant's allegations in this case cannot, and must not, be viewed in isolation from his detailed depiction of the circumstances in which such offending is said to have occurred. It cannot legitimately be said that no matter how probable the complainant's account might be, at *least in relation to matters of detail, and no matter how cogent the body of exculpatory evidence led at the trial might appear, the complainant's demeanour in the fact of sustained cross-examination must invariably trump factors of that kind.*

1101. In the case, as with so many others involving historical sexual offending, the devil is in the detail. It would be wrong to say that although the complainant may have been mistaken about the number of matters surrounding the commission of these alleged offences (as he unquestionably was) the jury, acting reasonably, might simply put all of that to one side, and dismiss mistakes as nothing more than matters at the periphery. Sometimes an approach of that kind may be justified. It does not, however, absolve this Court from its duty of carrying out a full and proper assessment of the whole of the evidence, including matters of detail. It is, after all, often only the details of an alleged offence that can be the subject of productive cross-examination. A verdict of guilty in circumstances where these matters cannot be properly probed, or explored, would and should be a matter of concern.

1112. Mine is, of course, a minority view in relation to ground one. I am troubled by the fact that I find myself constrained to differ from two of my colleagues whose opinions I always respect greatly. That has caused me to reflect even more carefully upon the proper outcome of this application. Having done so, however, I cannot in good conscience, do other than to maintain my dissent.[1]

---

1 Court of Appeal judgement – Pell v The Queen [2019] VSCA 186 – 21 August 2019 (Hearing 5 and 6 June 2019).

The Special Leave Application

On 17th September 2019 (with one day to spare) an application for special leave to appeal to the High Court was filed on Cardinal Pell's behalf.

A report in *The Australian* newspaper the following day (18 September 2019) contained the following quotation from the Application for Special Leave:

> *The majority concluded that if any of the evidence showed impossibility, in one respect or another, then the jury must have had a doubt.*

> *The facts as found by Justices Ferguson and Maxwell were that the only time when the room was empty for 5 to 6 minutes was a time when the complainant and the other boy, on the Crown's case were not in the room. Thus, according to this aspect of the majority's own approach the verdicts were impossible.*

> *Belief in the complainant is the beginning of the enquiry, not the end, they said. Belief is a prerequisite to conviction, but belief does not preclude the existence of a doubt raised and are left by other cogent evidence.*

> *To find otherwise would fundamentally alter the burden and standard of proof in the criminal trial and increase the likelihood of miscarriages of justice.*

In the same edition of the newspaper, Chris Merritt wrote:

> *Without a skerrick of emotion or one wasted word, Walker has torn the guts out of the Court of Appeal majority who rejected the Cardinal's appeal against conviction for sexually assaulting choirboys ... Walker is widely regarded as one of the nation's greatest lawyers. Yet his signature appears at the end of a document that accuses Ferguson and Maxwell of effectively reversing the onus of proof, engaging in 'unorthodox reasoning', 'circular reasoning' and erroneous judicial method.*

...

Whoever loses this argument will forever be damaged goods.

But as things stand now, Walker and Shann have the better argument.

It does look as though the cardinal has been the victim of a shocking miscarriage of justice.

(John wrote the above prior to the High Court granting Special Leave. However, it was his view that he agreed with what had been said by Chris Merritt above)

Reporting in *The Australian* newspaper in an article published on 14 March 2020 Associate Editor John Ferguson wrote the following:

Cardinal Pell's last chance comes down to a matter of minutes

'Kerri Judd had a dark day in the High Court on Thursday.

Victoria's Director of Public Prosecutions stood at the Bar table in Court One grappling for hours with what looked like an unbearable weight in the case against George Pell.

It is impossible to say with certainty how the High Court will respond to the Prosecutor, but her performance was marked with tense exchanges and at times what looked like exasperation from the Bench. It is now a live possibility that the High Court will intervene and free Pell, ending his six-year jail term one year in'.

'Judd's oral submissions tell the story of the problems confronting the prosecution, fundamentally on the key question of time and therefore the opportunity for Pell to have offended in the Priests' sacristy at St. Patrick's Cathedral in Melbourne in 1996 and 1997.

Judd has conceded the prosecution could not say specifically how long the complainant took to get to the sacristy after mass, how long the offending lasted and when the private prayer time ended.

These facts are crucial to whether or not Pell could have had time to molest the two choirboys, as found by the jury, raising further questions about probability. As a result, the shadows lengthen over the jury verdict'.

...

'The evidence was not such that it left no opportunity for the offending to occur,' Judd submitted to the Court. At one particularly embarrassing point, Chief Justice Susan Kiefel castigated the QC who was lamenting the sheer weight of material she had to deal with in trying to inform the Court.

Kiefel told Judd it was her role to take the Court through the case, adding: 'You're supposed to be taking us through it efficiently.'

Judd's problem, it must be said, seems to have little to do with her general legal ability and much to do with a case that looks hard to defend in the sharp light of the High Court'.

...

'Pell's closest supporters are quietly confident that he will soon be freed although mindful of the multiple setbacks since he was charged in June 2017. That confidence is shared by other legal experts, fuelling speculation he could be out of the Barwon prison in weeks.

If that happens, it will be a tremendous blow to the prosecution, at the same time as igniting what will be one of the great culture wars in modern Australian history'.

The judgment of the High Court delivered on 7 April 2020 in this matter is, in my respectful opinion, a refreshing one not just because it is a unanimous judgment of all seven Justices of the High Court, but also because it is written in language that, it seems to me, is readily understood by laypeople as well as by lawyers.

It is also a somewhat cumbersome document (128 paragraphs). It would be tiresome to read it all to you today, but those of you who are interested and have the time to do so might find it an interesting read. I would just like to read to you the following (which occurs towards the end of the judgment).

> 118. It may be accepted that the Court of Appeal majority did not concur in holding that A's evidence of the first incident did not contain discrepancies, or display inadequacies, of such a character as to require the jury to have entertained a doubt as to the guilt. The likelihood of two choirboys in their gowns being able to slip away from the procession without detection; of finding altar wine in an unlocked cupboard; and of the applicant being able to manoeuvre his vestments so as to expose his penis are considerations that may be put to one side. It remains that the evidence of witnesses, whose honesty was not in question:
>
> i. Placed the applicant on the steps of the cathedral for at least 10 minutes after mass on 15th and 22nd December 1966
>
> ii. Placed him in the company of Portelli when he returned to the Priests' sacristy to remove his vestments; and
>
> iii. Described continuous traffic into and out of the Priests' sacristy for 10 to 15 minutes after the altar servers completed their bows to the crucifix.
>
> 119. Upon the assumption that the jury assessed A's evidence as thoroughly credible and reliable, the issue for the Court of Appeal was whether the compounding improbabilities caused by the unchallenged evidence summarised in (i), (ii) and (iii) above nonetheless required the jury, acting rationally, to have entertained a doubt

as to the applicant's guilt. Plainly they did. Making full allowance for the advantages enjoyed by the jury, there is a significant possibility in relation to charges 1 to 4 that an innocent person has been convicted.

The significant words in passage 118 above are 'whose honesty was not in question' and 'rationally' for it is not sensible or rational or fair to say to a jury that they might act on the evidence of the complainant notwithstanding its inconsistency with the evidence of other witnesses. Where witnesses are called and questioned and no suggestion is made that they are wrong, it is a very odd thing indeed that the jury should be asked to disregard their evidence.

What follows further below under the heading, 'How Could Things Get Worse' was written before I had seen *The Australian* newspaper of 20 September 2019. Chris Merritt, a journalist I have come to admire, wrote under the heading 'Pell's accuser had treatment for psychological problems', that Pell's application for special leave makes it clear that the cardinal's accuser had suffered from psychological issues that had required treatment.

Further, he says that the defence team, and in the absence of the jury, sought approval from the trial judge to obtain records outlining this man's psychological problems, but were rebuffed. He says the judge had little choice due to the impact of Section 32D of the Evidence (Miscellaneous Provisions) Act which he said, 'skews the balance in favour of those who allege they are victims of sexual assault'. That is because there are very limited circumstances in which documents/information of the type sought can be made available to defence lawyers.

As he goes on to say, this is particularly important in a case where there is uncorroborated testimony relied upon and accordingly credit looms large.

As he says, allowing the defence lawyers to explore the medical records would have enabled questions such as whether the complainant had ever suffered from delusions and whether his psychological problems have resolved to be explored.

He further points out that while this might seem insensitive, 'with a man's liberty at stake, a bruising time in the witness box is no big deal'.

I don't know how anyone could disagree with that.

The Victorian Act is worth a look.

By Section 32B, 'protected evidence' is defined to mean evidence that is protected from being produced or/and used by Section 32C(1).

Section 32C provides that a party to a legal proceeding cannot compel another party to produce a document containing confidential communications. Further, evidence is not to be adduced in a proceeding if it would disclose confidential communication or the contents of the document recording confidential communication unless the Court grants leave to compel the production of the document or to produce it or to adduce the evidence and the party seeking to have the document produced or to produce it has given notice of their intention to do so in accordance with the sections.

Section 32D says the court must not grant leave to compel the production of or to produce or adduce protected evidence unless:

... it is satisfied that the evidence will either by itself or having regard to other evidence produced or adduced by the party seeking leave have substantial probative value to a fact in issue at hand;

and that other evidence of similar or greater probative value concerning the matters to which the protected evidence relates is not available;

and the public interest in preserving the confidentiality of confidential communications and protected health information and protecting a protected person from harm is substantially outweighed by the public interest in admitting into evidence of substantial probative value.

Psychiatric Issues

Chris Merritt, writing in *The Australian* on 8 April 2020, said:

The worst aspect of this case is that Victorian legislation meant the Pell jury was denied the full story about the man who claimed to have been assaulted by the Cardinal.

Relevant evidence about the complainant was kept from the jury by virtue of legislation that was put in place with the clear intention of protecting those who claim to be victims of sexual assault.

The Pell jury was never told that the complainant had a history of psychological problems that required treatment.

Nor were they told that Pell's legal team was rebuffed in Court – in the absence of the jury – when they attempted to gain access to records showing the extent of this man's psychological problems.

That episode is outlined in the Special Leave Application that was filed in the High Court by Pell's legal team, led by Bret Walker SC. During the trial, it would have been a contempt of Court for anyone to reveal this incident.

No part of the High Court proceedings was televised so it was not possible to watch that and to form an impression as to how things were going from the point of view of either side.

How Could Things be Worse?

We could be living, as do lawyers in New South Wales, with Section 293 (now section 294CB) of the Criminal Procedure Act. That section provides:

> *(1) This section applied to proceedings in respect of a prescribed sexual offence.*
>
> *(2) Evidence relating to the sexual reputation of the complainant is inadmissible.*
>
> *(3) Evidence that discloses or implies:*
>
>> *a) That the complainant has or may have had a sexual experience or a lack of sexual experience, or*
>>
>> *b) Has or may have taken part or not taken part in any sexual activity, is inadmissible.*
>
> *(4) Subsection (3) does not apply:*
>
>> *a) If the evidence:*
>>
>>> *i. Is of the complainant's sexual experience or lack of sexual experience, or of sexual activity or sexual activity taken part in by the complainant at or about the time of the commission of the alleged prescribed sexual office, a hand*
>>>
>>> *ii. Is of events that are alleged to form part of a connected set of circumstances in which the alleged prescribed sexual offending was committed,*
>>
>> *b) If the evidence relates to a relationship that was existing or[1] recent at the time of the commission of the alleged prescribed a sexual offence being a*

---

1   Section s294CB of the Criminal Procedure Act.

relationship between the accused person and the complainant,

c) *If:*
   i. *The accused person is alleged to have had sexual intercourse (as defined in Section 61H(1) of the Crimes Act 1900) with the complainant, And the accused person does not concede that the sexual intercourse so alleged, and*
   ii. *The evidence is relevant to whether the presence of semen, pregnancy, disease or injury is attributable to the sexual intercourse alleged to have been had by the accused person,*

d) *If the evidence is relevant to:*
   i. *Whether it at any relevant time there was absent in the complainant a disease that, at the time of the alleged prescribed sexual offence there was present in the complainant a disease that, at any relevant time, was absent in the accused person or*
   ii. *Whether it at any relevant time there was absent in the complainant a disease that, at the time of the alleged prescribed sexual offence, was present in the accused person.*

e) *If the evidence is relevant to whether the allegation that the prescribed a sexual offence was committed by the accused person was first made following realisation or discovery of the presence of pregnancy or disease in the complainant (being a realisation or discovery that took place after the commission of the alleged prescribed sexual offence),*

f) If the evidence has been given by the complainant in cross examination by or on behalf of the accused person, being evidence given in answer to a question may, pursuant to Subsection 6), be asked

g) And if the probative value of the evidence outweighs any distress, humiliation or embarrassment that the complainant might suffer as a result of its admission.

(5) A witness must not be asked:

a) To give evidence that is inadmissible under Subsections (2) or (3), or

b) By on behalf of the accused person, to give evidence that is or may be admissible under subsection (4) unless the Court has previously decided that the evidence would, if given, be admissible

(6) If the Court is satisfied:

a) That it has been disclosed or implied in the case for the prosecution against the accused person that the complainant has or may have, during a specified period or without reference to any period:

   i. has sexual experience, or lack of sexual experience of a general or specified nature, or

   ii. had taken part in, or not taken part in, sexual activity of a general or specified nature and

b) the accused person might be unfairly prejudiced if the complainant could not be cross-examined by, on behalf of the accused person, in relation to the disclosure or implication, the complainant

> may be so cross-examined, but only in relation to the experience or activity of the nature (if any) so specified during the period (if any) so specified.
>
> (7) On the trial of a person, any question as to the admissibility of evidence under subsections (2) or (3) or the right to cross-examine under Subsection 6 is to be decided by the Court in the absence of the Jury.
>
> (8) If the Court decides that the evidence is admissible under Subsection (4), the Court must before the evidence is given, record or cause to be recorded in writing the nature and scope of the evidence that is so admissible and the reasons for that decision.
>
> (9) (repealed).[1]

This extraordinarily complicated piece of legislation is difficult to take in one sitting. However, it may be accepted that it operates to exclude evidence which may be broadly described as evidence relating to the complainant fabricating sexual assault and assault complaints against males on the trial of a man charged with rape and other sexual assault offences.

The Weekend Australian newspaper (7–8 September 2019) carried a story concerning a trial against an alleged rapist 'RB' and asserting that the Judge in question urged the Director of Public Prosecutions to reconsider a decision to press on with a rape trial in which 'the alleged victim has a long history of fabricating sexual assault complaints'.

'He (the DPP) is presenting that witness to the jury as an honest witness ... Ultimately the (DPP) may want to look at this case ... Knowing full well on a previous occasion she (the alleged victim) has pleaded guilty to making a false account to the police.'

---

1   See R v RB: Attorney General (SW) as Intervenor 2019 NSWDC 368 (2 August 2019).

Afterthoughts

Two very interesting pieces appeared in *The Weekend Australian* newspaper on 11–12 April 2020. They were both published on the same page, which was headed 'Travesty of Justice'.

Paul Kelly (the newspaper's editor-at-large) said:

The George Pell story is a fiasco that combined incompetence and malevolence. It had every aspect of tragedy – a big man who polarised opinion, a church engaged in criminal behaviour, victims who demanded justice, and police, media and legal institutions that failed to honour their obligations.

It is a particular Australian tragedy that originates in the horrific crimes of the Catholic Church. These crimes and their coverups were worse than normal crimes because they ruined the lives of children and violated the raison d'etre of the Church – to proclaim God's mission.

...

This week's High Court decision brought a certainty and finality to this dismal saga of many years. Its essence is its 7-0 unanimity. There can be no further argument. Pell was wrongly convicted and jailed for 404 days. He is no longer the 'convicted paedophile', as his opponents loved to brand him.

The High Court reached this decision not by resort to activism or inventing new law but by invoking the core principle of the criminal justice system – guilt must be established 'beyond a reasonable doubt'. The decision did more than release a man wrongly convicted who was likely to die in prison. It provided the defining interpretation of the Pell fiasco. It offered – along with the minority judgment of Mark Weinberg in the Victorian Court of

Appeal – the lens through which the multiple institutional failures in the Pell case can be seen and assessed.

It is Pell's opponent who broke the conventions and retreated from legal reasoning. It is Pell's opponents who fomented a mood bordering on irrational vindictiveness that meant he was denied fair process. The High Court's repeated use of the word 'rational' in its judgment is revealing in its logic – that Pell was treated in an irrational way by the justice system.

This is polite judicial language. Let's call it for what it was: a sentiment in part of the community that Pell's trial had a meaning transcending guilt or innocence – that he must be punished for the Church's crimes in the name of its hundreds of victims. This is how many saw his trial, and, in this sense, it was a political trial.

Only the High Court, in its wisdom, halted the abuse of the justice system. The force of its judgment raises the inevitable question: if the case had been treated on its merit Pell would not have been charged. The evidence was inherently implausible.

We live in a time of institutional failure, demonstrated in our financial, political and religious systems. Sadly, institutional failure can beget more institutional failure. This has happened in the Pell saga in relation to Victoria police, the Director of Public Prosecutions, the Victorian justice system and much of the media with the ABC conspicuous for its sustained campaign against Pell.

These institutions are compromised. In each case they failed to meet their responsibility. These failures should neither be denied nor suppressed. Each contributed to a situation where Australia's most senior Catholic and the most senior figure in the Church worldwide to face such accusations was convicted as a sexual predator, with huge cultural and moral consequences if this conviction had been upheld.'

In an article called 'Pell's sad saga of suffering' in *The Weekend Australian* on 11 April 2020, Father Frank Brennan said:

> The problem with the Pell case from the start was the way in which it was handled by the Police. For some months, the office of the Director of Public Prosecutions tried to get the Police to improve the Brief of Evidence. The police then decided to go it alone and charge Pell on Summons. With a lack of due diligence, the Police failed to interview possible key witnesses.

The police told the media:

> Advice was received and sought from the office of the Public Prosecutions; however ultimately, the choice to charge Cardinal Pell was one that was made by Victorian police.

> John Champion, who was DPP at the time, said his office would conduct the criminal proceedings. From then on, the office of the DPP went to extraordinary lengths trying to cobble together a case. This was the second problem. Once the trial process commenced, the DPP kept shifting ground all the way up to the High Court promoting a case inconsistent with the evidence.

> What does it mean for society to believe Mr "A" in the way the Prime Minister indicated? It should mean that when "A" presents as a complainant to police, he is treated respectfully and sensitively, while he pieces together his traumatic memories of past assaults. The police did this, and they did it well.

> Commendably, Victoria police has worked closely with victims groups and their lawyers. While police were listening respectfully to "A" they should still have been

committed to orthodox investigation, collecting evidence consistent with "A's" account, and scrutinising any evidence consistent with his account. The police should then have gone back to "A" pointing out how his honest recollection of past events did not tally with the evidence of the routine practices in the Cathedral – evidence that could have been provided to the Police by perfectly decent, honest people doing their best to recall what they routinely did in a highly organised liturgical setting more than 20 years before.

A solemn mass with an Archbishop in attendance in St. Patrick's Cathedral is a bit like a military parade when it comes to discipline and ritual. The Police did not even make the most rudimentary enquiries of those who knew like the back of their hands, the procedures for a solemn mass.

"A" alleged that he and his friend, "B" were assaulted for 5 to 6 minutes by Pell after mass in the Priest's sacristy when the sacristy door was unlocked and open, and when there were no other persons in the room. It's important to note that there are three sacristies in the Cathedral: The Archbishop's sacristy, the Priest's sacristy and the workers sacristy which is also called the utility room.

The DPP told the High Court Pell would ordinarily have used the Archbishop's sacristy to robe and disrobe. But Pell did not ordinarily use the Archbishop's sacristy before 1997. In fact, there was no evidence that Pell had ever used the Archbishop's sacristy for disrobing before 1997. He used the Priest's sacristy which was also frequented by any Priests participating in a mass, as well as the altar servers when attending to sacred vessels, ferrying them back from the sanctuary. Priests don't go into the workers sacristy, where altar servers disrobe and attend to things such as candles, flowers and incense.

The startling gap in the Police investigation was their failure to interview alter servers and other key people who were routinely in the Priest's sacristy.

"A" also alleged a second attack by Pell a couple of months later in the corridor of the Cathedral when there would have been 40 to 50 people standing beside Father Brendan Egan, who had just said mass. "A" never mentioned the later assault to his friend "B". I won't complicate the story by saying anything further about the assault as Sergeant Christopher Reed, the lead investigator, admitted neither he nor any other police undertook any investigation of this allegation, and for whatever reason they never even spoke to Egan who, though no longer a Priest, still lives and works in Melbourne.

The Weekend Australian of 18–19 April 2020 was still giving significant coverage to the saga. Chris Merritt wrote what I thought was a very unfair criticism of Justice Maxwell of the Court of Appeal in Victoria (on page 11 of that publication) under the headline: 'Pell Appeal Judge's shock admission: "I'm no criminal lawyer"'.

The basis for the story was that in November 2002 (17 years ago) when Justice Maxwell was the immediate past president of Liberty Victoria, he gave evidence at a senate enquiry into proposed counterterrorism laws along with one Gregory Connellan who had succeeded him as the head of Liberty Victoria. The writer told us that the Hansard record recorded the then Mr Maxwell telling the senate enquiry, 'As I was president when we sent in our submission, Greg and I will deal with the issues together. Greg is a criminal lawyer, which I am not.'

The writer did not attempt to deal with what might have happened between November 2002 and the date on which the judgment was given in the Victorian Court of Appeal in respect to Cardinal Pell's appeal.

Whilst it is perhaps interesting to know that whatever experience Justice Maxwell had of the Criminal Law was probably gained in the main between 2002 and 2019, it was a disappointingly sensational headline.

All one could say is that it was a little curious that the majority Judges did not pay attention to Justice Weinberg's judgment, bearing in mind that he is widely recognised as one of the most experienced criminal lawyers in the country.

A much more interesting story appeared (on page 20) where a reporter named Angela Shanahan reported that the 'news' of a new investigation into historic sexual assaults involving Cardinal George Pell was being pursued by the Victorian police. She said:

How can they now deny an irrational "get Pell" agenda?

The case against the Cardinal should not have even been prosecuted because the Magistrate in the committal hearing who sent the Cardinal to trial, noted: "If a jury accepted the evidence of Monsignor Portelli and Mr. Potter (the sacristan) ... then a jury could not convict."

Angela Shanahan also drew attention to another case involving a high-ranking catholic prelate.

Max Davis, she said, was the Catholic bishop of the Australian Defence Force. He had a long and distinguished career and was well thought of by ordinary soldiers because he had been to various areas of deployment, including Afghanistan.

She told us that in June 2014, Davis was charged with having indecently assaulted a 13-year-old boy in 1969 (45 years before). The one complainant, she says, was followed by more and eventually there were six counts related to the period between December 1968 and October 1972. Davis had been a young teacher and a dorm master at St Benedict's College, New Norcia.

The charging of Davis was sensational as, until Pell, he was the highest-ranking prelate charged with this offence.

But what happened next well illustrates the problem of shifting the onus of proof. All the victims swore that their abuser was Davis, that he was one of the brothers, even describing the famous Benedictine habit. However, contrary to the testimony, Davis was a layperson – he was not ordained until 1971 and he was never in the Benedictine order. Davis left the school in the later 1960s and went into the seminary and was ordained in 1971. While he was at the school he was not 'Brother Max' as was claimed, he was simply Mr Davis. The trial became a fiasco when it became clear the police had not checked the enrolment records at the school at the same time as Davis was there. One of the accusers was not even enrolled at the relevant time.

Eventually, the defence, and Davis himself, accepted that some of the boys were abused but it was a case of mistaken identity. Davis was acquitted of all charges in February 2016 and although he returned to public ministry in December 2017, he has battled to properly clear his name since that time. The media was almost silent on his acquittal, his working with children clearance was withheld, the army treated him with great disdain and he feels that this will hang over him for the rest of his life.

I must say that I had not heard of this case until I read Angela Shanahan's article. But there can be no doubt that if what she says is true or even largely true it is a shocking indictment of the failure of the Victorian police to make a proper investigation before laying charges calculated to attract media and public attention.

No one should be subjected to this sort of treatment by a legal system that prides itself on ensuring that innocent people are not wrongly prosecuted and/or wrongly convicted.

PART 8

A Properly Funded Legal Aid System

We live in what I think is a profoundly unhappy society. There is a great imbalance between the poor in our society and the moderately well-off, let alone the wealthy.

In Peter Robinson's book *When the Music's Over* the author describes a community in the estates in the United Kingdom as follows:

> *This ... is what becomes of certain people when they feel disenfranchised, get put down and ignored all the time and come to feel there is no useful way through life for them, that nobody cares and nothing is going to change for the better. The most extreme ... sit catatonic in their chairs day in, day out. For the rest there are drugs, drink, violence, crime or just simply apathy broken up by the distraction of videogames, sex and mobile phones. Life is something to be got through. Days are hurdles, weeks are rivers to cross, months lakes, and years oceans.*

Increasing parts of Australia are like that I think and there is little point fighting elections about making things better for multinationals, for working people for families while we do not address this very major problem.

A United, Collegiate Profession – Do We Have a Lot to Learn From the Americans?

Whether from Americans or others, we do have much to learn. The legal profession has become a business where profit is more important than principle and the billable hour is the driving consideration.

'No Win, No Fee' advertising is now common and combined with the extra pressure placed on practitioners whose practices are incorporated means that the interests of the injured plaintiff is often not at the forefront of the practitioner's mind when settlement offers are being considered.

It should not be thought the penniless plaintiffs were not previously assisted by the profession. I know of cases in the pre-advertising days (fortunately, not many of them) where the costs of the unsuccessful litigation were borne by the practitioners and no attempt was made to recover them from the unsuccessful plaintiff. It was a system that was not broken and did not require fixing.

Time Costing and Budgets

Time costing and fee generation budgets put enormous pressure on the young practitioners of the modern era.

During the time that I was the leader of the Bar in Townsville, I spoke with many bright young lawyers who were driven out of private practice and sought government employment to remove that pressure from their lives. I was sad to see them go as they were the ones the profession needed.

Others coped by artificially building up time estimates, which is easy enough to do, particularly in complex matters where such a thing would pass unnoticed, but it's nonetheless dishonest.

Judicial Officers Returning to the Fray

It has become increasingly common in recent years for judicial officers to retire, receive payments of a very generous judicial pension, and then return to work in legal roles.

I have been a voice against this ever since I was appointed a judicial officer.

My view of things is that the judicial pension exists and is justified on one basis and one basis only. That is that judicial officers are not vulnerable to bribes or other undue influences because from the moment of appointment, their position is secure and they will not have to curry favour with anybody for the rest of their lives.

As with the age pension, the judicial pension was probably introduced at a time when it was not anticipated that lengthy retirements because of changes in life expectancy, would be a problem.

However that may be, it seems to me that those who wish to return to active legal practice after their retirement should forego the pension or at least a portion of it equivalent to their earnings in private practice.

One of the first to engage in this practice was Sir Laurence Street, who became a very prominent mediator after his retirement from the New South Wales Court. I was never involved in a mediation in which he was involved but I heard from others that years of judging left him quite unable to mediate. Nonetheless, he was popular and commanded extraordinary fees for his service as a mediator. Ian Callinan QC was to follow a similar path after his requirement from the High Court. Many others would follow. Some Queensland judges were able to supplement the judicial pension by accepting appointments as acting judges in New South Wales.

It is not only the question of money that makes this an objectionable practice. It is also the fact that those who engage in it trade on the fact that they have been judicial officers as if that somehow makes them better or more valuable consultants, legal practitioners or mediators.

Those who have experienced their efforts will tell you that years of making decisions often do not help a person to be a useful mediator as the practice of mediation is quite different to the practice of judging.

It is, I think, foolish to imagine the government will just continue paying judicial pensions to former judicial officers who are practising as lawyers or charging significant fees and generating significant income by acting as mediators, legal consultants and the like.

The public should not be expected to bear the burden of making the wealthy wealthier where there is no benefit to the community.

This objectionable practice began, like most objectionable practices in my legal experience, in New South Wales, but quickly spread to Queensland, where it was enthusiastically taken up and continues to this day.

The December 2017 edition of the *Lawyers Weekly* recorded (on page 34) that Michael Kirby and Gillian Triggs, who were described as 'human rights champions', had been appointed as the inaugural patrons of the Refugee Advice and Casework Service (RACS). I was a great admirer of Michael Kirby's during his long judicial career but it seemed to me that there must be a measure of desperation driving one who still wants to be publicised so much that he would be prepared to be photographed in company with Gillian Triggs, whose main claim to fame as far as I could tell was that she behaved entirely improperly in respect of the prosecution of claims against some students who were bold enough to suggest that there was an element of discrimination being practised in a university that reserved computer facilities for the use of Aboriginal students only.

Perhaps the day will come when the judicial pension scheme is reserved for payment to *retired* rather than *former* judicial officers. Another suitable remedy might be to require an accounting and credit for income received from those who wish to supplement the judicial pension with other earnings.

The solution to all this might be found in assistance being offered to retired judicial officers to cope with and accept the fact that with retirement comes diminished importance and diminished 'respect' (real or imagined) and diminished status in the community.

Whether any of this will work remains to be seen.

Accurate Reporting of Court Proceedings

Townsville has always been poorly serviced for newspaper reporting. I don't know whether the *Townsville Bulletin* was the newspaper that prompted someone to refer to newspapers as 'rags', but it could well have been.

When I first came to Townsville an effort was made (at least in my view) to convey to the public what actually happened in court.

I'm not going to dwell on this but simply quote a recent example of entirely inaccurate reporting designed (calculated) to mislead and deceive.

On Friday, 8 September 2017, two things occupied the front page of the *Bulletin*, apart from an advertisement for real estate. Almost half the page was taken up by the *Bulletin's* campaign to persuade people to subscribe to the *Bulletin*, as a 12-month digital subscription would entitle the subscriber to a pair of Sennheiser wireless noise-cancelling headphones. I will not dwell on this.

The other half of the front page was a story concerning a legal case under the headline: 'Rape Mum Walks Free'.

The first paragraph of the story confirmed the headline with these words:

> *A woman who helped her boyfriend rape her daughter on the girl's 12th birthday has walked free from Court after admitting to the 'horrific' crime.*

Many readers probably would have stopped reading at this point, the story confirming their view that the legal system was failing the community. Those who followed the direction on the front page to read the rest of the story on page 5 would have found a slightly less attention-grabbing headline: 'Rape Mother Avoids Jail'.

It is only those who persisted to the final paragraph of the article on page 5 who would have learned this:

> *Judge Dorney sentenced the woman to 5 years jail for the rape and three years jail for the indecent treatment charge, with both sentences to be served concurrently and suspended immediately for five years.* **Meaning the woman will not serve any time in jail for the offences.** *[emphasis added]*

Well, what's wrong with that?

1. First, a person who is sentenced to imprisonment, wholly suspended, does not 'walk free'. The suspension is conditional upon the person sentenced not committing any offence punishable by imprisonment within the operational period specified (in this case five years). If the person sentenced does commit such an offence within the operational period, then that person carries the onus of satisfying the Court that it would be unjust to require any of the sentence be served.

2. Second, it will be obvious from what I have already said that a suspended sentence of imprisonment does not mean that the person sentenced has 'avoid(ed) jail'.

3. Third, it will be obvious from what I have already said that it is a little premature to say, when reporting the sentencing proceeding, that the person sentenced 'will not serve any time in jail for the offences'.

Judges know these things. Lawyers know these things. Persons who sit in Court and listen to the proceedings will hear the judge explain these consequences to the person being sentenced. No person with a modicum of intelligence attending the sentencing procedure could go away thinking that what happened was that the person sentenced 'walked free' or 'avoided jail'.

The reporter in question might escape responsibility for the headlines, which, as I understand, are written by sub-editors whose attention might be expected to be more focused on circulation figures than accuracy. However, the reporter cannot escape responsibility for the last paragraph of the report, including the assertion that the suspension of the sentence means that the person sentenced 'will not spend any time in jail'.

All who contribute to stories like this, which occur with monotonous regularity in the *Townsville Bulletin*, know or should know that they are feeding the public misleading and deceptive information. If it happened once, one might say it was an unhappy accident. When it happens time after time, one can only conclude that it is deliberate.

A hard marker might also expect that competent reporters would know that the judge referred to would correctly be described as 'Judge Dorney QC' rather than 'Judge Dorney'.

But perhaps I expect too much.

That the problem persists is illustrated by reading the *Townsville Bulletin's* front page of 8–9 August 2020.

There, under the heading 'Parole for Wife Basher', a person named Cameron Bates recorded that a former Virgin Australia pilot who had bashed his wife in front of their two young children 'has walked free from the Courthouse'.

Again, one has to read the whole of the story to find that the magistrate in fact jailed the man for 18 months but released him on immediate parole. Anyone who thinks that a man sentenced to 18 months imprisonment but released on parole 'has walked free' must have gained a significant part of their education from the *Townsville Bulletin* rather than any sensible source of legal information.

It is not just the community that requires some legal education – persons permitted to write reports about legal proceedings ought to be required to have some basic understanding of what they are doing.

The Business of University Education

In recent times, universities have switched their attention from 'homegrown' students to the more profitable overseas market where students with plenty of funds are plentiful.

In the case of students who are classified as having refugee status, it is not even necessary, at the James Cook University at least, for the student to pass an English test before being enrolled in a degree course. The universities churn out graduates, many of them with an indifferent understanding of the areas in which they have qualified.

Professor Ridd and the James Cook University of North Queensland[1]

This case was said to be about intellectual freedom or academic freedom. That is a concept sent to independent universities and institutions devoted to higher learning.

The trial Judge in this matter said:

In reality intellectual freedom is the cornerstone of this core mission of institutions of higher learning. This is so because it allows ideas to conflict with each other; to battle and test each other. It is within this 'battle' that strengths and weaknesses of ideas are found out. In this process, there comes 'learning'. And with learning comes discovery.

At its core, intellectual freedom mandates that academics should express their opinions openly and honestly, while inviting scrutiny and debate about those ideas. Unless opinions are expressed in this way, the growth and expression of ideas will be stifled and new realms of thinking will cease to be explored that will lead to intellectual and social stagnation and a uniformity of thought which is an anathema to the concept of higher learning and social progress.

It is difficult to disagree with any of that. Yet what happened to Professor Ridd demonstrates that these values are at risk at the James Cook University.

It seems Professor Ridd had been concerned with the quality of scientific research that had been published about the state of health of the Great Barrier Reef. He had published a number of papers on the need for better quality assurance.

On 16 December 2015, he sent an email to Peter Michael, a journalist with News Limited. In effect, this

---

1   (2019) FCCA 997.

email suggested that reports regarding the degradation of the Great Barrier Reef by sediment were not reliable. Overall, the email was critical about the methodology used and the conclusions made. The email even suggested questions that Mr Michael might wish to pursue with the organisations responsible for those reports.

Mr Michael sent the whole email to a Professor Hughes and asked for his comments. Professor Hughes wrote to Professor Cocklin making a complaint about the fact that Professor Ridd had written to Mr Michael. Professor Hughes characterised the email of Professor Ridd as one that was 'spun' and claimed it attacked his integrity and that of the institution generally.

The matter was investigated and Professor Ridd was given a formal censure and a 'direction' as to how he was to conduct himself in the future. He subsequently wrote an essay questioning the conclusions about the degradation and damage to the Great Barrier Reef and as a result, was invited to appear on a television program.

Professor Hughes contacted Professor Cocklin and Professor Harding complaining about this.

In August 2017, Professor Ridd was contacted by the HR manager for the university, who alleged there was a case of serious misconduct committed by him. On 21 November 2017, James Cook University found that Professor Ridd had breached the code of conduct, denigrated Professor Hughes, denigrated the university, interfered with the disciplinary process and breached confidentiality.

He was given a final censure and again a direction regarding confidentiality.

Professor Ridd had already commenced proceedings in the Federal Court but it is not clear that the university knew that at the time. Professor Ridd started a GoFundMe page to ask for donations for legal expenses.

On 13 April 2018, the university wrote to Professor Ridd and determined that nine further allegations of breaching confidentiality directions, breaching directions and breaching the code of conduct had been substantiated. The letter indicated that termination was appropriate but that the final decision would be made by the vice-chancellor.

On 2 May 2018, the vice chancellor terminated Professor Ridd's employment.

In the judgement that I have referred to, a judge of the Federal Circuit Court of Australia determined that the university had acted unlawfully. He invited the parties to make submissions on the issue of declarations and penalties and adjourned the matter for them to do so.

In September 2019, the Judge awarded $1.2 million to Professor Ridd.

The university retained one of Australia's leading advocates, no doubt at significant expense, to contest the initial findings and the award of damages.

Drew Pavlou and the University of Queensland

This student became famous overnight because he organised a protest against the Chinese government. This protest is said to have led to violence and death threats as well as disputes within his own university.

An article about him in *The Weekend Australian* magazine[1] describes him as 'a certified, card-carrying member of generation "Z"'. He is a mild-mannered eldest son of a conservative Greek greengrocer. His paternal grandparents migrated to Australia in the 1960s. The family made their way to the Gold Coast, opening fruit and vegetable shops, hairdressing salons and a restaurant. Drew was born to Nick and Vanessa in 1999. The family moved to Brisbane two years later.

---

1   Written by Matthew Condon and published in the magazine accompanying *The Weekend Australian* of 30–31 May 2020.

He attended the Villanova Catholic College for his high school years. He thinks of himself as a person who has always had a difficult relationship with authority.

Early June 2019 was the 30th anniversary of the Tiananmen Square massacre. Pavlou, who had never organised a protest before, felt an urge to do something about it. He decided to do it on the University of Queensland's market day. He knew that thousands of people would be at the university on that day.

Problems began the night before. Pavlou had posted details of the protest on 24 July on Facebook. Opponents started moving in before any banner had been raised or any words spoken. He received threats. He found and posted an insult to those who threatened him. They responded with death threats.

On the day in question, he slept in and after visiting the library to make up posters and print off flyers arrived about 30 to 40 minutes late.

There were lots of people waiting.

Pavlou and his small team of protesters sat down together to air their grievances, unaware that the crowd surrounding them had grown to upwards of 500 people. The protesters were declaring that they didn't want the university to do deals with the Chinese government. They bemoaned the plight of the Hong Kong protestors. They chanted that the Chinese president 'had to go'.

Then the violence began. Some think that the pro-China activists who instigated the violence were not students but rather 'trained heavies', possibly agents of the Ministry of State Security.

In November 2019, the university issued a statement about the university, its transparency and its commitment to freedom of speech and gave brief details about its investigation into the 24 July protest. It posed the question: is UQ committed to freedom of speech?

It answers its own question 'The events of recent months show that UQ is absolutely committed to freedom of speech. It is a fundamental tenant of any democracy and goes to the heart of the pursuit of truth, and therefore knowledge.'

Pavlou saw an opportunity to pursue the matter and campaigned for election as a UQ senator. He won.

On 9 April 2020, Pavlou received a 186-page document entitled 'disciplinary matters'. It detailed 11 allegations of misconduct, ranging from bullying to failing to show respect and courtesy in online communications. At the disciplinary hearing, Pavlou was represented by a long-time defender of free speech, Tony Morris QC. The confidential hearing was held on Wednesday, 20 May. Morris's 53-page response was powerful.

Pavlou had been expelled from the university for two years, a period which, curiously enough, would expire shortly after the conclusion of his term on the university senate.

The newspaper I have referred to, in its editorial of the same weekend, had the following to say:

The punishment, imposed late on Friday by the faceless disciplinary panel behind closed doors, says little about Mr Pavlou. But it says a great deal about the depths to which a powerful section of the once-great Group of Eight institution has sunk. Disgusted alumni can only wonder what distinguished vice-chancellors of the past, such as constitutional lawyer and former governor general Sir Zelman Cowen and literature scholar John Hay, who built the University's strength in scientific research, would think.

Even the University is embarrassed. An hour or so after the verdict chancellor Peter Varghese, a former secretary of the Department of Foreign Affairs and Trade stepped into the role of 'video umpire'. Mr. Varghese said he was personally concerned about 'aspects of the finding and the severity of penalty'.

...

In a style reminiscent of the CCP, the disciplinary panel gave no reasons for its decision. Its silence, for now, leaves Mr Pavlou's claim that the University acted to protect its business interests with the CCP unchallenged.

An extraordinary meeting of the university senate was called to discuss the matter.

The Curse of Advertising

For most of my practising life, it was not only unfashionable but also regarded as unethical, that lawyers should advertise their wares as if they were in business rather than practising a profession.

Alas, all that is gone now in the name of competition.

Advertisements by dental practitioners and lawyers dominate the evening news broadcasts and do not provide any real assistance to the person who might be seeking legal or dental advice as to where to seek it.

It does not seem to me that the professional life of either group has been improved or that service to the public has been improved by this innovation.

The Cheating Culture

Cheating has become endemic in our society. Protests fall on deaf ears. No amount of talking seems to result in action that will deter the culture.

I will say a little more about this when dealing with body corporate life, where cheating is rampant and body corporate owners are victims who often feel quite powerless to act effectively against the cheats.

PART 9
Body Corporate Living

Body corporate living causes great frustration to many thinking people in Queensland. It seems to me that that is largely because of inadequacies in the legislation and ignorance of the people who carry on business as body corporate managers as well as those who live in body corporate environments.

I do not hold myself as having great expertise in respect to body corporate matters, but I have had a deal of experience.

My first encounter with the body corporate was in respect of the Aquarius building on The Strand in Townsville. Since then, I have also had experience with One Bright Point (Magnetic Island) Body Corporate, the Yarrawonga Village (Townsville) Body Corporate and the body corporate for Altitude in the city of Townsville.

Whilst most of the experiences have been unhappy ones, I must say that a spirit of cooperation makes all the difference and the body corporate at Yarrawonga Village in the time that I was involved with it proceeded without any major dissatisfaction or unhappiness.

The same cannot be said for any of the others.

The Queensland legislation is, in my view, unnecessarily complicated and difficult to understand. Most people who live in these body corporate environments have an extremely limited understanding of the powers and duties of the body corporate and its committee.

Several basis propositions need to be understood.

First, an owner of a unit in a body corporate owns the unit and shares in the common property. The unit owner is not exempt from liability and/or responsibility for things that occur on the common property.

Second, the body corporate committee is no more than a selection of representatives of the owner to carry on the day-to-day business of the body corporate. It is not a separate entity but is more akin to a group of directors of an incorporated company who have responsibilities to their shareholders.

Third, the owners of units would be much better served by the body corporate being kept to a body corporate for a reasonably limited number of units. I have had dealings with bodies corporate where there are 140 to 150 units involved. That is, in my opinion, far too many to be managed by a committee that is limited by the legislation to having only seven members.

Fourth, the body corporate environment is a place where it is likely that factions will develop and people will seek to advantage themselves, sometimes to the disadvantage of other owners. Sometimes they act honestly, believing that what they are doing is within the powers and/or for the benefit of all. At other times they overestimate their powers and/or deliberately set out to advantage themselves, either through ignoring a conflict of interest or downright dishonesty (dishonesty is always a risk).

All these matters need to be addressed and, in my view, they need to be addressed by a significant overhaul of the legislation being undertaken and by the establishment of something akin to the current commissioner's office but something that has real teeth and a real interest in carrying out its functions.

I had occasion to contact the commissioner's office once in respect of an insurance issue that arose at the One Bright Point units. After three months, an extremely helpful person at the commissioner's office was able to tell me that I had filled out the wrong form and that if I wished to take the matter further, I should start again with a different form.

This is behaviour calculated to drive people away and to leave unit dwellers in an unhappy situation where they cannot get useful help or advice without committing themselves to significant legal expenses. I know the unscrupulous trade on this by telling people repeatedly that we must avoid consulting lawyers because it is so expensive. The problem is that they need to understand that it is a question of consulting lawyers or just putting up with what the loudest mouths dictate.

The legislation is crying out for a significant overhaul. It has received an overhaul of sorts in Queensland, but the serious faults remain.

It seems to me that as the number of people living in units grows, the dissatisfaction felt by them and the pressure for reform can only increase.

We would all be much better off if prospective members of a body corporate committee were required to take some form of training about the responsibilities and duties that committee members have.

It seems to me that many of them think, as I have pointed out, that they govern rather than serve.

The Joy of Taking Offence and Political Correctness

"The West is facing three barbarians: militant Islam, Russia and China. The enemy within the gate is the new religion of political correctness, with its first commandment, 'Thou shalt not offend'. If you want to keep something you believe in, sometimes you have to fight for it. None of the Western world's present leaders are prepared to do that".[1]

> *There are a great many victims in our midst, all of them worthy of our attention and support; victims of natural disasters, of illness, of relationship breakups, of retrenchment, of prolonged unemployment leading to poverty and yes, even of incompetent, neglectful or abusive parents. In whatever situation they find themselves, victims are entitled to expect a compassionate response from us. But the person who embraces the role of victim and wears it like a badge of honour is a person in need of a different kind of help.*[2]

The Australian newspaper of 21 November 2017, contained an article concerning the entertainer and comedian Barry Humphries (page 3). It began:

> *Barry Humphries knows all about outrage. If he is blessed with a gift, he says it's the gift of giving offence.*

He said that he had watched people become, in recent years, 'touchier than ever'.

Bill Elton, a comedian who took on the British establishment in the 1980s, wrote:

---

[1] Jim Wilson, retired schoolteacher, in a letter to the Australian Newspaper published 18 February 2016.

[2] Part of an edited extract from 'The Inner Self – The Joy of Discovering Who We Really Are' by Hugh Mackay, published in The Weekend Australian's magazine 8–9 August 2020.

'The Enlightenment, when suddenly the light of reason shone through humanity's natural predilection towards suspicion, superstition and bigotry, gave us democratic government, the rule of law and the notion that you had to support your position with empirical evidence,' he said.

'In the last 15 years, in my opinion almost entirely because of the internet, it is all in play again and people are choosing their own truth, their own facts, their own science, their own evidence and finding massive communities for this.

'This is much more f..king serious than whether a bunch of comics are making jokes that have outraged the student union in Leicester,' he said.

'What Twitter has done to the public debate is terrifying and possibly terminal. There is more to discuss in terms of the cancel culture than a bunch of millennials feeling rightly sensitive about what they see as important identity issues.' [3]

'Terminal' is probably a good word to use, particularly when one reads of the establishment of *The Journal of Controversial Ideas*, set up by Peter Singer, a Professor of Philosophy at the elite Princeton University in the United States, Jeff McMahon of Oxford University and Francesca Minerva of the University of Ghent. The idea of the journal is to allow researchers to publish peer-reviewed articles under fake names so as not to risk their careers or suffer intimidation on social media.

Perhaps it's a good idea but it's also an indication of how far the chattering classes have destroyed sensible discussion of matters of public interest.

Anyone who thinks that these statements rather overstate the position should have a look at Michael Sexton's book *Dissenting Opinions*.

---

3   *The Australian* newspaper 18 April 2021.

A collection of stories that illustrate this problem follows:

The Townsville Bulletin Again

On 4 November 2017, the *Townsville Bulletin* contained a headline on page 16:

Hate Book Led to Loss of TCC Job

The article was written by Andrew Backhouse and read as follows:

A former Townsville City Council employee who was suspended for six months after leaving an incendiary book at work claims free speech is at risk if same-sex marriage legislation is passed.

William Engelbrecht was the subject of a serious misconduct investigation by the council after leaving the book in his workplace lunchroom with his business card and name written inside.

The book, *Correct, Not Politically Correct – How Same-Sex Marriage Hurts Everyone* by Frank Turek, argues strongly against same-sex marriage. Mr Engelbrecht said he inadvertently left the book in the council lunchroom. Another council employee found it and a complaint was made, sparking months of legal wrangling that eventually led to downgraded misconduct charges and a suspension from the council.

According to the council, the book contained material that was considered to incite hate and have a serious contempt for or to severely ridicule others on the grounds of their sexuality.

Mr Engelbrecht has since accepted a voluntary redundancy. Now he is warning that reading an alternative opinion against the mainstream views on same-sex marriage could result in legal action.

'Legalising same-sex marriage will not only undermine the very essence of what marriage is about, a union between a man and a woman in order to raise well-adjusted children, but will severely impact our right to have an alternative opinion or even to debate an alternative opinion,' Mr Engelbrecht said.

A Townsville City Council spokesman said, during mediation with the Queensland Industrial Relations Commission, that it agreed 'that Mr. Engelbrecht had engaged in misconduct by leaving inappropriate material in a workplace.'

My research reveals that Frank Turek has a website called *Cross-examined* and expresses Christian views and has written otherwise than in the book complained about.

If it is accepted that the book was left in the lunchroom inadvertently, found by another employee and read without permission, surely Mr Engelbrecht was more sinned against than sinning.

I am told that sometime later, some form of apology was published in the *Townsville Bulletin*, but I have not been able to locate a copy of that.

The South Australian Statue

The Australian newspaper of 23 November 2017 contained (again on page 3) a story concerning a statue erected at a school in Adelaide which was thought to be 'potentially suggestive'. It was said that the statue of Saint Martin handing a young boy a loaf of bread was of an 'unintentionally provocative design' because the loaf of bread was 'phallic-looking'.

The article was accompanied by two photographs, the first showing the saint, the boy and the loaf of bread and the second showing the statue draped in dark material (perhaps resembling a burka).

For the Term of my Legal Life

The previous day's edition of the *Adelaide Advertiser* dealt with the same story under the headline 'Sorry Saint Dominic we need a cover-up'. That story occupied about one-half of the page and whether by accident or deliberately, the balance of the page was a story under a headline 'Police on watch for toolies'. It seemed to me that both stories warranted inclusion in this writing lest it be thought that I am making things up.

In another section of this book ('The Business of University Education'), I mentioned what happened to Professor Ridd of the James Cook University and Drew Pavlou of the University of Queensland. I need not repeat the things I have said about those men and the appalling treatment they received simply for having a view that did not suit the universities with which they were involved.

We really do have cause to be concerned.

PART 10

Regrets, I've had a Few

Note to the reader. John had a number of titles for this section but did not complete it so I have listed them.

- *Attempts to establish inclusive chambers*
- *A Bar Association with little or no regard for the work of real lawyers concerned with the liberty of the subject*
- *The establishment of a separate Court of Appeal.*
- *The Moynihan reforms*
- *Tort reform*
- *Advocacy*

Acting for Friends and Family

I was persuaded to do this on a number of occasions. I must be a slow learner because I was not put off by the fact that time after time my efforts on behalf of family and friends were not appreciated.

1. **John Riley** was the man who introduced me to Christine, and he arrived in Townsville to work about the same time that we did. When he asked me to act for him in a dispute he was having with his employer, I had no hesitation as we had always been friends. One thing led to another and on another occasion, I acted on his behalf in Cairns. By this stage, I thought he was becoming very intense, but it turned out later that he had a brain tumour and I expect that accounted for his behaviour. We obtained what I thought was a pretty good result in the litigation, but he somehow convinced himself that I had aligned myself with our opponents and somehow done him out of his rightful compensation. Things were very unpleasant for a time and it was only after his death that his children explained to me that he had been impossible to deal with for some years. One of the children was kind enough to arrange a helicopter flight to Magnetic Island and Chace and I went on to inspect the development at One Bright Point, Nelly Bay. It was a lovely day out and I took it to be a family expression of regret about the way in which our relationship had come to an end.

2. **James Todd Bradshaw** was a barrister I had known in New Guinea. When I met him, he was a very nice man and he was very kind to Christine and her mother (when her mother was visiting the Territory). When we had all returned to Australia, he took up practice in Cairns and his behaviour seemed to become a little erratic. He did not form a lasting relationship with a female for some years, and when he did, he formed one with a female who was herself very erratic in her behaviour. I

suspect he lost a great deal of money trying to defend her in litigation in which her case had no merit at all. He was driven to write some unwise and threatening correspondence to his wife's landlord and that led to him being in trouble with the Bar Association.

I told him that I thought that he should stick to criminal work because that was where his skills lay, and I did my best to arrange for him to have a practising certificate that was limited to criminal work. Members of the Bar Council accepted my suggestion readily because although James was very much at fault in respect to the complaints made about him, he was generally well-liked by other barristers and no one wished to see him without a practising certificate at all. I was on the point of confirming this arrangement, on his instructions, when he had a change of heart, rang me and accused me of all sorts of disloyalty and dishonesty and said he was going to write some letters himself. He did not actually sack me but when I saw what he had written to the Bar Association, I invited him to do so. By the time I did that, I think he could see the writing on the wall and was not keen to sack me. In the end, our relationship was greatly damaged, and I have not seen him for a very long time but I understand that he still resides in Cairns.

3. **Brice and Harkness** – These two friends of mine were jointly engaged in a plan to subdivide land at Horseshoe Bay on Magnetic Island. Harkness was a solicitor and Brice an engineer.

I was persuaded to appear in the Planning and Environment Court on the basis that I would not be paid unless their appeal succeeded. Their appeal was unsuccessful, significantly because Brice insisted that because he had engineering qualifications, he could give the necessary engineering evidence himself. I cautioned him against that and tried to explain to him that what was required was an independent opinion.

He would not listen. My fallback position was that if he insisted on giving evidence himself, he should at least turn up looking like an expert. Sadly, he had little respect for courts, lawyers and judges and turned up in an open-neck shirt, no jacket and his sleeves rolled up to the elbow. It was clear that the Judge did not like him and did not like his attitude.

The appeal was duly lost.

To rub a bit of salt into the wound, Mrs Brice informed me at a social function that she did not believe that I did not get paid as when they got the bill from the solicitors (a firm in which Harkness was, if not the senior, one of the senior partners) it was so large that she was convinced that there were hidden fees for me contained in it. I suppose all that can be said about that is that she shared her husband's view of where the centre of the universe was and thought that everyone else was dishonest when things did not go their way.

It was only when she told me that that I realised that I was the only person involved whose remuneration was dependent upon success. Silly me.

4. **My Sister, Louise** – My sister was very shabbily treated by the Tasmanian health system. Just about 20 years later, after she had endured appalling deprivations and loss of quality of life, she received what was then the largest award of damages ever made against the Tasmanian Government.

I had a great deal to do with the case because I had an idea that the Tasmanian lawyers were finding it all a bit beyond them and my brother had a view that it could not be settled in Tasmania because nobody at Treasury would sign off on the amount of funds required.

My sister, although she had a rather limited understanding of what was happening, was from time to time a bit stressed about the whole thing and took to referring to me as 'the smart-arse bastard'. I was pretty pleased with my input into the case as I know that unless I had intervened, it would have been settled for less than half of what was ultimately awarded.

It was just a shame that the stress of it all destroyed our relationship.

ABOUT THE AUTHOR

I was born in Geelong on 21 February 1947. I am a member of the Tasmanian branch of the Baulch family but I happened to be born in Geelong because my father was teaching at the Gordon Institute (now the Deakin University) and pursuing a football career with the Geelong Football Club.

That should be sufficient to explain my lifelong fascination with the Geelong Football Club.

I was educated in Tasmania attending the following educational facilities:

- Lansdowne Crescent primary school, West Hobart, Tasmania. (1953)
- Bowen Road Primary School, Moonah, Tasmania. (1954 – 1955)
- Charles Street primary school, Launceston, Tasmania (1956 – 1958)
- Devonport High School, Devonport, Tasmania. (1959)
- Queechy High School, Launceston, Tasmania. (1960 – 1962)
- Hobart Matriculation College. (1963).
- University of Tasmania. (1964 – 1968)

I completed a law degree in 1968 and graduated on 2 April 1969.

On 3 February 1969 I was admitted and enrolled as a barrister and solicitor of the Supreme Court of Tasmania.

On 30 January 1970 I was admitted to practice as a barrister and solicitor of the Supreme Court of the territory of Papua and New Guinea.

On 2 April 1973 I was admitted to practice as a barrister and solicitor of the High Court of the Western Pacific.

In January 1974 I was admitted to practice as a solicitor of the Supreme Court of Queensland.

On 18 July 1977 I was admitted to practice as a barrister of the Supreme Court of Queensland.

I have been a member of the American Association for Justice (formerly ATLA) since 1996.

I was the chairman of the Patient Review Tribunal, (Northern Region), between 1992 and 2002.

On 17 November 1998 I was appointed Senior Counsel.

I was a member of the Mental Health Review Tribunal during 2002.

I was a member of the Misconduct Tribunal between 2003 and 2008.

Adjunct Professor, Advocacy Courses at James Cook University 2009 to 2021.

On 10 September 2010 I was appointed a Judge of the District Court of Queensland.

I retired from the District Court on 20 February 2017 having reached the compulsory retiring age.

Following my retirement from the District Court I was appointed Queen's Counsel.

FORMALITIES
Swearing In

DISTRICT COURT
CHIEF JUDGE WOLFE
JUDGE DURWARD SC

IN THE MATTER OF THE SWEARING-IN OF JUDGE J R BAULCH SC
AS A JUDGE OF DISTRICT COURTS
TOWNSVILLE

DATE 10/09/2010
THE COURT RESUMED AT 9.36 A.M.

JUDGE BAULCH: Chief Judge, I present a commission appointing me a Judge of the District Court of Queensland.

THE CHIEF JUDGE: Let the commission be read.

COMMISSION READ

THE CHIEF JUDGE: Pursuant to the authority granted to me by the Governor of Queensland in accordance with section 59 of the Constitution of Queensland 2001, I now ask Judge Baulch SC to take the oath of allegiance and office.

OATH OF ALLEGIANCE AND OF OFFICE ADMINISTERED

THE CHIEF JUDGE: Yesterday, his Excellency, the Acting Governor, issued a commission appointing John Richard Baulch SC, a Judge of the District Court of Queensland. We convene here today not only to witness his Honour duly taking his oath of allegiance and office but so that the legal profession and the people of North Queensland may join with us in congratulating Judge Baulch on his appointment. I note with pleasure the presence of Justice Moncrieff of the Family Court, Federal

Magistrate Coker and Magistrates from this State Magistrates. I also note the presence of the former Registrar of this Court, Mr Ray Keane and it gives us all particular pleasure to note the presence here today of former Judge Pat Shanahan who practised for many years in this city and indeed, both as Judge and Chief Judge, frequently sat in this courthouse and its predecessor. It's a great honour to have you here today.

We regret that the northern Judge is on leave and so cannot be here with us today but Justice Cullinane asked me to especially mention his best wishes and those of his wife, Anne. Obviously, the Chief Justice cannot be here in Townsville with us today either. He is sitting in Court and as you would have heard when the commission was read, he is presently Acting Governor. The Attorney-General deeply regrets that he is in Brisbane today because of pre-existing commitments that he just could not get out of and he asked me to publicly express his congratulations to Judge Baulch and also the Government's congratulations and to wish Judge Baulch the best in the future as a Judge of this Court. The Attorney-General greatly appreciates Judge Baulch's willingness to accept this important office.

The Attorney-General also appreciates very much that the appointment of a District Court Judge to be based here in Townsville is an important occasion not only for the legal profession in Townsville and the broader regional area but also for the community and he is sincerely regretful that he cannot be here today and I know he really wanted to be here. Other Judges of our Court are of course wishing they could be here today and wish to be associated with the welcome we extend Judge Baulch. In particular, the Judge Administrator, Judge O'Brien, who began his judicial life on the Bench here in Townsville, especially regrets he is unable to be here today and he asked me to extend his particular good wishes to your

Honour as did another Judge who used to be based here, Judge Wall QC.

The number of practitioners and well-wishers here today is a wholehearted endorsement of the appointment of Judge Baulch to the District Court of Queensland. Members of the Judge's family are here today, and we include them and other distinguished guests in our welcome. Judge Baulch now joins our senior Townsville Judge, Judge Stuart Durward SC, in this important and busy city. Although District Court Judges have sat on and off in Townsville since 1870, Judge Baulch is only the 12th Judge to be appointed to serve the District Court with chambers here in Townsville since the District Court was reconstituted 51 years ago.

With valuable experience based in Papua New Guinea and Tasmania and as a solicitor in Townsville, Judge Baulch began private practice at the Bar in Townsville in 1977 and his legal experience is particularly fitting for this office. He has practised from chambers in Townsville since 1977. He was awarded silk in 1988 and in his 33 years at the Townsville Bar he has practised largely in the fields of commercial and insurance law, equity, tort, and appearing in the High Court, the Federal Court, the Court of Appeal as well as the Supreme Court, the District Court and I note, the Planning and Environment Court. He has also had a deep interest in alternate dispute resolution, a topic dear to the heart of every Judge. It will become dearer to your heart the longer you sit, Judge Baulch.

Importantly, Judge Baulch's chairmanship of the Northern Region Patient Review Tribunal, his presidency since 1999 of the North Queensland Bar Association and his membership of various community groups demonstrate Judge Baulch's commitment to the people of North Queensland. He comes to a Court, a Bench of 37 full-time serving Judges. Our 38th

Judge is practically full-time at QCAT, so we really needed Judge Baulch.

He fills the retirement, as you know, a few months ago of our 10th Townsville Judge, Judge Robert Pack, who also deeply regrets he cannot be here today and asked me to mention his good wishes and those of Wendy, his wife, to Judge Baulch. He is somewhere in the wilds of Goondiwindi today, I think.

We are relived that Judge Baulch has been appointed because we were concerned that without a second Judge here, the efficiency of the District Court, especially in Townsville, might be impeded. So, we are grateful with Judge Baulch's appointment and as you can see how grateful we are, we've wasted no time in swearing you in, Judge Baulch.

Judge Pack was farewelled - unfortunately I could not be here - in this Courtroom on the 18th of June and it is fitting, because I was unable to come on that occasion, that I recognise Judge Pack's service today. In his years on the Bench he was universally admired and respected as a Judge and as a person. As a Judge he had an unswerving adherence to the right to a fair and public hearing by a competent, independent and impartial tribunal established by law. As a person, his judicial life clearly illustrated those qualities of honour, courtesy and generosity of spirit to which we all aspire.

His absence I very much note. He was a great support to me, and I miss his wise counsel as well as missing his companionship and that of his wife. As the eighth Townsville Judge and now the Judge Administrator, Judge O'Brien said at Judge Pack's valedictory, "The very qualities that mark Judge Pack's time as a Judge were his profound sense of fair play and his deep understanding of his fellow human beings bringing to this Court the qualities of humility and of humanity which any Judge could do well to emulate."

Now, with Judge Baulch, we see a wealth of experience as a successful barrister in silk, the exact qualities needed to excel as a Judge of this Court with its vast jurisdiction. We therefore receive Judge Baulch with a strong sense that his appointment to this Court is one which the Judges and practitioners and importantly, members of the wider community here in Townsville and elsewhere in Queensland can be most confident. We wish you and your family well, Judge Baulch.

Mr Collins?

MR COLLINS: If the Court pleases, the president of the Bar Association of Queensland, Mr RJ Douglas of Senior Counsel, has asked me, as a regional representative on the council of the Bar Association, to represent him and the association today. On behalf of the members of the Association of Queensland, I welcome your Honour's appointment and recognise that you are a worthy appointee to this Court. Your Honour was admitted as a barrister and solicitor of the Supreme Court of Tasmania in 1969 and after a period of time working in Tasmania and then Papua New Guinea, your Honour came to Townsville to work as a solicitor in 1974. Your Honour's last call to the Bar was in 1977.

In your Honour's 33 years of practice as a barrister, you obtained a wide experience over many areas of the law. Despite your busy practice as a barrister, you served as the chair of the Patient Review Tribunal Northern Region from 1992 to 2002 and as a member of the Mental Health Review Tribunal in 2002 and a member of the Misconduct Tribunal after that. Your Honour has a reputation for a thorough analysis of the law. Your Honour's learning in the law was recognised in 1998 when you were appointed senior counsel. You have served as the president of the North Queensland Bar Association and have been a regional representative on the council of the Bar Association.

Your Honour brings to this Court a commitment to advocacy and you have been involved in advocacy training through the Australian Advocacy Institute for many years. Yours is the 91st appointment to the District Court since its reconstitution in 1959. It is pertinent to note that your Honour is the ninth District Court Judge to be appointed to the Bench from practice in Townsville. With a degree of pride, we in Townsville claim a further five Judges of the District Court as our own due to their practice here in their formative years. Mr Douglas and the council are deeply committed to the Bar in regional Queensland as is your Honour.

Your Honour's appointment is a further recognition of a robust and capable Bar throughout regional Queensland. The Bar Association of Queensland thanks you for your service to the association, wishes you well and we look forward to working with you in your new role as a Judge of the District Court. May it please the Court.

THE CHIEF JUDGE: Thank you, Mr Collins. It is a pleasure to see you here this morning, a former acting Judge of our Court, one of many who in that role have given so much to the public through such service. You have many alumni like Justice Kate Holmes of the Court of Appeal who started her judicial service as an acting Judge of this Court. So, we're very glad that you could speak for the Bar this morning. Mr Mackey?

MR MACKEY: Thank you, your Honour. With great pleasure and on the behalf of the President of the Queensland Law Society and the solicitors of Queensland that I welcome and congratulate your Honour on your elevation to the District Court Bench.

It is a particular pleasure because I am familiar with your Honour's consistent and enthusiastic support of the profession and young practitioners in North Queensland since I arrived here as a solicitor 31 years ago.

You have been instrumental in arranging seminars and doing workshop educationals and promotion and presenting papers at the North Queensland Law Association conferences. The appointment of your Honour as a local practitioner is regarded by the profession as most appropriate. It is noted that as a consequence of your appointment the absence of a senior counsel at the local Bar, a position the local profession hopes will be rectified shortly.

My friend has been brief on details in respect of your exploits in North Queensland, and I believe that is an excellent precedent to follow in this forum. I know I talk for my colleagues when I say you have the total support of the profession.

THE CHIEF JUDGE: Thank you, Mr Mackey. Judge Baulch?

JUDGE BAULCH: Thank you, Chief Judge. Chief Judge, Judge Durward, Mr Collins, Mr Mackey, my special friends in the jury box, ladies and gentlemen. Thank you all for attending, for the very kind things that you have said about me this morning. I have to resist the urge to look around to see who the person is that's the subject of all this praise because it doesn't feel as if it should be me.

I've had a very fortunate life in the law. My early years were supervised by three lawyers, whose influence I feel to this day, and I will mention them to you for it, and it will give you an idea of the background that I had.

My last year of study was a part-time year of study and I was fortunate to serve as associate to Mr Justice Chambers of the Tasmanian Supreme Court. After admission I obtained employment in New Guinea in the office of the Public Solicitor of the then Territory of Papua New Guinea. The Public Solicitor then was a man called Peter Lalor, a former patrol officer who had an encyclopaedic knowledge of the laws of the Territory, the product of study at night by the light of a kerosene lamp, and a great knowledge and understanding of the country's people.

Later in Tasmania I spent some time employed as Crown counsel in the office of the Crown Advocate, then Mr Henry Cosgrove, later Mr Justice Cosgrove, of the Tasmanian Supreme Court.

Three more different men it would be difficult to imagine. Mr Justice Chambers was a shy, retiring man who kept very much to himself. Peter Lawlor was given to coming into the office in volley sandshoes without laces. He didn't own a tie and only occasionally wore a belt. Henry Cosgrove was an outgoing fan of horse racing and racetracks and the son of a former Premier of Tasmania. But those three men shared one quality; they loved legal practice and teaching others, particularly young practitioners, about the law and legal practice. To those three men I owe a great debt, for they provided support and encouragement, and more importantly understanding when things weren't going so well in my formative years.

By the time I came back to the Bar in Townsville in 1977 I felt able to conduct a criminal trial without embarrassing myself, and that was due to the assistance that I'd received from those men. I was fortunate, I think, to have their assistance and guidance at a time when the financial returns of legal practice did not dominate legal life as they do today.

So how then does a university student from Tasmania finish up in Townsville? When I was working in the Territory a former Chief Judge of this Court, Pat Shanahan, has been appointed a District Court Judge in Queensland and accepted an acting appointment to come to New Guinea. I appeared before him for a number of miscreants in Rabaul and was very taken with his sense of justice and his ability to relate to what was a completely new environment for him. We went out on my speed boat one day and stopped at the Pigeon Islands, which are outside the mouth of the Rabaul harbour and one of the most beautiful places that I have ever been.

We had to stop at the island and bring the boat ashore because it was necessary to build up our fluids again in the heat, and we sat on the beach and he told me about his time in Townsville and the wonderful practice that he had had here and how he had enjoyed living here. I just soaked this up, never thinking that Townsville would be my place of residence.

Ted Lindsay had worked with me in Papua New Guinea in the Public Solicitor's office before returning to Townsville to practise with his brother, Richard, who had established a practice here in the early 1970s. I was then the Deputy Public Solicitor in Rabaul and I recall receiving several phone calls in which Ted encouraged me to come to Townsville and take up practice here. I remembered what Pat had told me of his life in Townsville and thought it might be worth a try.

Some of you will be aware that I did practise with the Lindsay Brothers for a time, and although solicitors' practice didn't have lasting appeal for me, Townsville did. Pat and Ted and Richard introduced me to Townsville, and I'm pleased they did, for without their influence I might never have come here.

Thirty-six years on I am committed to this community and I hope that I will end my days here. Some of you may wish to remonstrate with Pat and with Richard and Ted about their collective wisdom in encouraging me to come to Townsville. Those of you who do should wait until this proceeding is concluded to express your views.

I thank the North Queensland profession for their company, their friendship and their support. My life here has been rewarding and enjoyable because of that friendship and support. I am now at home whether in Townsville, Cairns, Mackay or Rockhampton. I know that some people have travelled from those centres to be here at short notice, and no doubt considerable inconvenience, and I'm very grateful to them for doing so. I hope that in my judicial life I will still feel at home in all of those centres, as I do here.

One of the very nice things about this occasion is that I see many non-lawyers sitting here and sharing the morning with me. I want to continue to be not just a lawyer in this community, but a friend of yours. Thank you all for coming.

I come now to the most important person here today - I say that with respect to the Chief Judge and Judge Durward - Christine.

THE CHIEF JUDGE: We know who you're speaking about.

JUDGE BAULCH: Christine has been a constant support for me. She's not only been a homemaker and a mother, but also the manager of my practice. Her success in those areas led her to briefly believe that she could also manage my life. This was the most difficult assignment for her, and whether she succeeded or not does not really matter, because the effort stood her in very good stead to manage the teenage years of our daughters. I think at times for her it was like having four teenagers to look after. In less than two years we'll celebrate 40 years of married life, and for me at least it will be cause for celebration. Christine has brought me children I love, and now grandchildren, who complete the picture. I cannot imagine life without her, and I fancy that but for her we wouldn't be here today.

Sadly, for Christine the day is not all positive. She sees herself losing her long-standing employment with an employer she's found both generous as to remuneration and the availability of holidays. In that employment, until today, she had felt secure.

The positive for me is that she will have much more time to devote to me.

I thank you all very much for attending. This is for me a special day, and such a large number of people attending makes me feel very honoured. I look forward to the challenges of my new position and to continuing to work with you as a member of the North Queensland legal profession. Thank you.

THE CHIEF JUDGE: Thank you, Judge Baulch. And thank you to all speakers this morning. I'm grateful for your very positive addition to today's ceremony. Now, there'll be morning tea in the jury assembly area, and of course all here are most welcome to join the Judge and his family and all of us there this morning.

Let these proceedings be recorded. Adjourn the Court.

THE COURT ADJOURNED AT 10.06 A.M.

FORMALITIES
Valedictory

DISTRICT COURT OF QUEENSLAND

CHIEF JUDGE O'BRIEN

NORTH J

IN THE MATTER OF THE VALEDICTORY CEREMONY FOR HIS HONOUR JUDGE BAULCH SC DCJ

TOWNSVILLE

10.03 AM, MONDAY, 20 FEBRUARY 2017

Any Rulings that may be included in this transcript, may be extracted and subject to revision by the Presiding Judge.

WARNING: The publication of information or details likely to lead to the identification of persons in some proceedings is a criminal offence. This is so particularly in relation to the identification of children who are involved in criminal proceedings or proceedings for their protection under the *Child Protection Act 1999*, and complainants in criminal sexual offences, but is not limited to those categories. You may wish to seek legal advice before giving others access to the details of any person named in these proceedings.

Also, Present:
On behalf of the Government of Queensland:

Mr Peter Dunning QC, the Solicitor-General of the Attorney-General's Department

Mr David Mackie, the Director-General of the Department of Justice and Attorney-General

On behalf of the Office of Public Prosecutions:
Mr Michael Byrne QC, the Director of Public Prosecutions

THE CHIEF JUDGE: Members of the profession, distinguished guests, ladies and gentlemen, we gather today to farewell a Judge who has served this Court and the people of this State with great distinction since his appointment on the 10th of September 2010. Among the many present to honour Judge Baulch today, we acknowledge the presence of the Northern Judge, Mr Justice North, and Mrs Jane Seawright, the honourable Kerry Cullinane AM, and Mrs Anne Cullinane, members of the Magistracy, the Deputy Mayor of Townsville, Councillor Les Walker, Mr Scott Stewart MP, the member for Townsville, the former Registrar of the Townsville Court, Mr Ray Kean, Mr David Mackie, the Director-General of the Department of Justice, Mr Rob White, the North Queensland Regional Director. Also present are the Director of Public Prosecutions, Mr Michael Byrne QC, and the Public Defender, Mr John Allen QC.

We note with particular pleasure the presence of retired District Court Judges, Judge Bob Pack and Mrs Wendy Pack KC, Judge Marshall Irwin and his wife, Louise, and Judge Brian Hoath and his wife, Denise.

We welcome also members of the Judge's family who are able to be here today: his wife Christine and his daughters Justine, Olivia and Chance and their families. As Judges, we know well the enormous contribution that families make in a Judge's life.

There are many who could not be here today but who have asked that their apologies be conveyed to the Judge. They include Judge Wall QC who contacted me last week with that request, the honourable Justice Peter Tree of the Family Court, Judge Coker of the Federal Circuit Court, the honourable Robert Monteith, formerly a Family Court Judge here in Townsville, Mr Graeme Crow QC of the Rockhampton Bar, Mr John Griffin QC. His association with Judge Baulch, of course, goes back to their time in New Guinea. Others, Mr John Taylor, Mr Gene Patterson and the Chief Magistrate, Judge Rinaudo.

Finally, in that regard, there are many of our own judicial colleagues who, by reason of distance and other Court commitments, are not able to join us today. All, however, have asked that their apologies and good wishes be conveyed to Judge Baulch. In a sense, many of them are participating in these proceedings as they are being streamed live to Courthouses in Cairns and Ipswich. It had been intended to stream them also to the Brisbane Courthouse, but events of the weekend, of which some of you at least may be aware, have caused some change in those plans.

Judge Baulch was born in Tasmania and was there admitted as a Barrister and Solicitor on the 3rd of February 1969. As he reminded me only the other day, he has recently celebrated the 48th anniversary of his admission to the legal profession, a truly impressive achievement.

He came to North Queensland via Papua New Guinea in 1974. He practised as a Solicitor before joining the Townsville Bar in 1977. It was around that time in the late 70s that I first him, and he was already establishing a name for himself as a formidable advocate. Later, in my nine years as a resident Judge in Townsville, I was able to observe and admire those skills much more closely.

He took Silk in 1998, and then in 2010, became the 12th Judge of the modern era to be appointed to sit in Townsville. He came to this Court abundantly well qualified for his new role. He had been Chair of the Patient Review Tribunal, was a Member of the Mental Health Review Tribunal, he had been involved in community activities, he had been President of the North Queensland Bar Association and had served as regional representative on the council of the Bar Association.

His practice at the Bar had been extensive, involving both criminal and civil work. During his time as a Judge, Judge Baulch has sat in all our court's jurisdictions – criminal, civil, appellate and planning – and he has done so with distinction. His decency and commitment to the delivery of justice according to law have been the hallmarks of his time on the District Court. In an age when alternative measures of dispute resolution became increasingly fashionable, Judge Baulch maintained throughout his strong belief in the entitlement of all citizens to have their disputes judicially determined in accordance with established principle.

He maintained also throughout his time on the Bench his interest in advocacy, advocacy training, establishing his involvement with James Cook University. He was ready always to offer advice and guidance to any young counsel in need of assistance.

He also managed, successfully, I think, to balance his judicial responsibilities with his interests in the Geelong Football Club, no easy matter for such a fervent supporter. Around the time of his appointment, he was quoted as saying that his greatest regret was that Geelong had won only four premierships during his lifetime. He retires in the knowledge that they have since won two, and if I am wrong in those numbers, I know that Judge Baulch will correct me.

He will be missed on this Court, but we wish both he and Christine well for a long and happy and, may I add, healthy retirement. He will, I know, relish the opportunity to spend more time with his family, particularly, perhaps, his grandchildren, and, of course, in lending his support to that other great love, the Geelong Football Club.

Mr Solicitor.

THE SOLICITOR-GENERAL: May it please the Court. Chief Judge, Judges of the District Court, retired Judges of this Court, particularly Judge Pack, Judge Hoath and Judge Irwin, Judge Cullinane, the former Supreme Court Judge here, Justice North, my colleagues, the Director of Public Prosecutions, Michael Byrne QC, the Public Defender, John Allen QC, the Director-General of the Department of Justice, Mr David Mackie, Stewart Scott, the member for Townsville, and Counsellor Walker, the Deputy Mayor of Townsville, Judge Baulch's family, distinguished guests all, I rise today on behalf of the Attorney-General, who I at once express her apologies, your Honour, for being unable to be present due to other work commitments. It is therefore my privilege to, on behalf of the Government, express its appreciation and thanks for your Honour's distinguished service on this Court.

The Chief Judge has carefully catalogued your Honour's nearly half-century career in the law, and I will avoid repeating what his Honour has said, but as we have heard, your Honour has practised from tip to toe on the east coast of Australia and into New Guinea and no doubt those days in New Guinea with the likes of Judges Hoath and Wall, as they became, with whom you practised, and nobody could take an experience with John Griffin QC without getting something out of it, must have honed your Honour for practise not only at the Bar in Townsville, but later as a member of this Court.

Resident Judges of the District Court and of the Supreme Court are a uniquely Queensland experience of the administration of the judicial arm of Government in the Commonwealth. They are not only unique, but they are uniquely advantageous. They provide ready access for justice in regional areas, they provide a career structure for local practitioners and, as we have already heard, they provide important mentoring for those practitioners. Yet above all of those laudable features of resident Judges in regions is the fact that resident Judges provide not only the appearance, but the reality that justice is administered by the local community, not to the local community. That is something that could only occur with the commitment of Judges like your Honour, who take an appointment to the Court, immerse themselves in the local community and make the discharge of their function something that the community feels a part of and on behalf of the Government, we thank you for that.

Your Honour, as we have already heard, has given service of great distinction to the North Queensland community. Your Honour came to the Court well placed, with a substantial practice in all of the areas of the law, but particularly in significant common law cases. Your Honour was at the vanguard of mediation as an alternative dispute resolution method while still at the Bar, with others to catch up.

Your Honour, as we have heard, has had a distinguished career on this Court. I am reliably informed by those who appear in that jurisdiction consistent with the practice in the north, your Honour has been astute to ensure that plaintiffs in personal injuries cases were, to the extent the law permitted, fully rewarded as far as money could.

Your Honour has also given considerable support to advocacy training in the north, not only through the Australian Advocacy Institute, but also the James Cook University, which really returns me to where I started. What your Honour has done, as your Honour's fellow Judges who appear in Townsville and elsewhere in the State, is given an approach to and a connection with the administration of justice in this State that is truly unique.

I take this opportunity of thanking you again, your Honour, for your contribution to the Court and wishing your Honour and your family a very happy phase in the next stage of your life. May it please the Court.

THE CHIEF JUDGE: Mr Hughes.

Christopher Hughes, president of the Bar, speaking at my Valedictory

MR HUGHES: May it please the Court. Chief Judge O'Brien, Judges of this Court both past and present, Judges, Magistrates and members of other Courts and Tribunals, again both past and Present, Solicitor-General, Ms Smyth, members of the legal profession and particularly my many friends practising in North Queensland, ladies and gentlemen, I came very willingly here this morning, though as I look about the room, I see that other heavy weights from the Queensland Bar also came willingly, but the Association has sent me here today not just as a mark of respect for his Honour Judge Baulch, but in recognition of the importance and the respect the Association places in and has for the regional Courts, the regional Bars and the regional Solicitors of this vast State.

If I echo some of the words of the Solicitor-General, it is because on those matters the Bar Association feels similar sentiments to the Government. The existence of more than a century of Supreme and District Courts in Rockhampton and Townsville, and more recently in Cairns, underscores the importance of the availability of immediate access to justice well beyond the south east corner.

The presence of and the work done by Judges in the regions, particularly, as the Solicitor-General said, those Judges resident in and forming part of the regional communities, cannot be underestimated, nor, Chief Judge, should it be unvalued. That is the view of my Association, which look forward to the Attorney-General moving to replace his Honour as soon as practicable, but that won't happen until his Honour shuttles off to the fairways and the cellars of North Queensland. I am only glad that my cellular is not in North Queensland, and I am only glad that I am unlikely to be in the four following his Honour on any fairway.

We are here today, however, not to agitate general matters or not to be flippant, but to celebrate and give thanks to the specific man's contribution to North Queensland. That said, it's not possible to deal with your Honour, and please forgive me, without reference to that diaspora of men of similar vintage who came from the south, and some from the very deep south, but after flirtations with exotic locations, such as those places famous for honing subtle and technical legal skills like New Guinea, Brisbane and even Roma, that diaspora settled to serve the interests of justice in North Queensland.

For the benefit of the Italian scholar Justice Cullinane, the Roma to which I refer is the one in South West Queensland and not the eternal city in Italy.

Putting aside the venerated Judge Pack, there were three from the deep south who brought with them in your Honour's group to Townsville a particular and some say peculiar interest in an odd game, an odd game particularly in Townsville, now the home of the Cowboys. Clive Wall, of course, came from Melbourne and eventually he developed, for admirable, parochial reasons, a like for the Brisbane Lions, formerly, of course, the Fitzroy Lions. Tony moon, who is one of my members who is here with us today, also came from Melbourne and who, curiously, constantly and tragically has been linked with the Collingwood Football Club, and your Honour came from even further south, from Tasmania, and for reasons unexplained, your Honour developed an unnatural affection for Cats, that is, the Geelong Cats. I understand your Honour's Chambers is decorated – or in the words of Moon, desecrated – with the Geelong paraphernalia, and I also understand from a mole in your Chambers, that your mobile telephone enjoys the ring tone of the Geelong Football Club, a song which, sadly, the young in the room have not had many occasions to hear over the last couple of years.

Indeed, your Honour's deep-seated affection for all things Geelong had many of my colleagues fearful that one day on arriving in your Honour's Court, we might see Gary Ablett sitting at your Honour's Associate's desk. Instead, of course, of recent times, we have seen Adria Askin – the very capable Adria Askin whom I had the pleasure of entertaining, and I use the word advisably, for work experience some years ago, and that, Chief Judge, is actually a segway, because the first time I met his Honour Judge Baulch was at the wedding of Adria's parents, Philip Askin, a well-known and some way likeable Townsville Solicitor, and the charming Christine Askin. I must say I have personally seen much of Mrs – Dr Askin's charm. I have seen precious little of Philip's likability.

It was at the wedding as a callow young counsel from Brisbane – this is back in 1983 – that his Honour I first met on a hot afternoon. But if meeting his Honour was a shock, can I ask you to spare a thought for me because on the same afternoon, I met Clive Wall, Bob and Wendy Pack KC, James Webb and the recently appointed Gill Trafford-Walker. The collective experience was such that I was so traumatised that I dared not to reappear in Townsville for almost a decade, but reappear I did and I have enjoyed enormously the camaraderie of the Barristers in Townsville, the briefs of some of the Solicitors in Townsville, although Moon says I am breaking his rice bowl, and the opportunity to come to Townsville over the years, Judge Baulch, I have had both the pleasure of appearing against and before you.

As many of my colleagues at the Bar will attest, the former was always a roller-coaster experience. Your Honour as an opponent was energetic, sometimes surprising, but always effective. In terms of the latter, when appearing before your Honour, your Honour was pleasant, good humoured, at times almost avuncular and always determined to shed the detritus and get swiftly to the real issues to be determined, not wasting time or energy on what your Honour saw as peripheral matters.

Indeed, my last appearance before your Honour gave your Honour the opportunity one last time to shine. Your Honour demonstrated sharpness, your Honour was to the point, your Honour was incisive, and your Honour was decisive, though some may say that these comments need to be tempered by the fact that the matter turned out to be a consent adjournment, but I saw different things that day, as did my opponent.

To paraphrase the classics, like many before you, your Honour came to the Townsville Bar. Your Honour liked what you saw and your Honour in your own way conquered it and then your Honour moved on, like many before you, and accepted the call to contribute to the well from which you had drunk and accepted appointment to this Court. In doing so, you joined the ranks occupied by many outstanding men, including Judges Finn, Ambrose, Hall, Hanger, Trafford-Walker, Wylie, Wall and Pack and, of course, the Chief Judge himself.

You leave behind you on the Bench alone, we hope only briefly, his Honour Judge Durward, who also has contributed so much to the Townsville community and to North Queensland, but there is more to be said about his Honour Judge Durward perhaps by someone else and perhaps next year when we may farewell him also.

Your Honour served on the Council of the Bar Association of Queensland, for which the members remain grateful. Your Honour has served this Court, this community, this city and this region well. Many of us are only too aware that your service may have been even greater, and certainly would have been more comfortable for you but for the recent health challenges which you, in your usual style, have taken in your stride.

Judicial careers are perhaps, sadly, cut short by statute, but friendships are not. You and Christine will take into your retirement the friendship and the best wishes of many of us – in fact, all of us – at the Bar of Queensland.

If it please the Court.

THE CHIEF JUDGE: Ms Smyth.

Christine Smyth speaking at my valedictory

MS SMYTH: May it please the Court. I am honoured to be here today to thank Judge Baulch for your long and distinguished service to the community and the legal profession. I am given to understand, though, that while at the Bar, your Honour sometimes made a point of noting that if more people attended a Judge's farewell than his swearing in, it was an indication that they were happy to see him go than they were to celebrate his arrival. However, as I look around the room, given your Honour's resumé, I think it is safe to assume that those here today do not hold your Honour's theory and are acknowledging your exceptional contribution to this Court and the community.

I emphasise a service to the community because, in essence, that is what a career on the Bench is. Lay people might simply think that the work of a Judge is another job and perhaps one which is automatically achieved at a certain point in a lawyer's career, but here at the coalface, we know how erroneous that is. Appointments to this honourable Court is an acknowledgement of superior legal knowledge, a capacity for hard work and a commitment to fairness and the rule of law as a facilitator of the society in which we live.

Discharging duties as a Judge of the Court means delivering justice and serving the community without being influenced by irrelevant factors and the vagaries of an often capricious media, ready to pounce on any decision which might capture the attention of the public. It also requires a versatility as the District Court is rightly regarded as the hardest working of the Courts, with a jurisdiction that encompasses everything from serious criminal offences and complex commercial matters to appeals in all manner of legal disciplines.

Your Honour has discharged these duties with admirable competence, as evidenced by your reputation throughout the profession as a scrupulously fair Judge possessed of great intellectual reader and genuine professional courtesy.

In researching this speech, the feedback on your Honour was – from the legal profession can be summed up, I believe, in the words that only North Queensland can provide: top bloke, not a bad word can be said about him. In Australia, no higher praise can exist for a man than the words top bloke, and perhaps it is fitting that we celebrate your Honour in the shadow of the Oscars, awards much prized by the acting community because they are voted on by their peers. Based on the regard in which your Honour is held by the rest of the profession, were it possible, you would be taking home an Oscar today.

Your Honour's resumé also reveals that you have not just been a Judge here in Townsville, but an enthusiastic and supportive member of the whole community through your involvement in the organisations such as Rotary and your enthusiasm, from what we have heard today, for exploring local golf courses.

Your Honour's commitment to giving back to the profession does you great credit, not just through organisations such as the North Queensland Bar Association, of which you were President, and by making yourself available for Queensland Law Society events, such as the North Queensland Symposium for which you have the Society's heartfelt thanks, but also for your willingness to pass on your vast knowledge to the next generation of lawyers and in that regard, your Honour established, with the Queensland Law Society member, Mr Terry Browne, who is here with us today, the James Cook University Advocacy course which regularly receives excellent reviews from its students. This is a subject near and dear to my heart as one of my focuses as President of the Queensland Law Society is to establish opportunities for instruction in advocacy for Solicitors. I may well seek your counsel on that one day.

I note also that your Honour has an interest in and has presented on legal ethics. No doubt that is a hangover from your origins in the ethical side of the profession, otherwise known as Solicitors.

Your Honour is also possessed of great loyalty, so we have heard today, of maintaining a love for the Geelong Football Club and for ACDC and so I have heard it is a long way to the shop if you want a Chiko Roll.

In closing, I know your Honour has done both your profession and your community proud through your career, and the Queensland Law Society and its members wish you all the best in your well-earned retirement.

May it please the Court.

With the Chief Judge at my valedictory.

THE CHIEF JUDGE: Judge Baulch.

JUDGE BAULCH: Thank you and pardon me if I do not recite the usual preamble. I know why there has been such a big turnout today.

It puzzled me for a while, but I thought you are probably all expecting that you would read my views about all sorts of legal issues in the *Courier Mail* last week, but you did not have that opportunity.

If you have come here expecting you are going to hear some radical reform talk today, I am sorry, you are going to be disappointed. I have some ideas about that, but I do not think that an occasion like this is the time to air them.

I am going to produce a memoir, perhaps, of my experiences, not just in Queensland, but in Papua New Guinea and the Pacific Islands. I know that one should not settle on a title too early because publishers or proof-readers might advise, but I had it in mind that a good title might be "Things I Found Out" because I have found out a few things over the years.

So, if you want to know anything, you will have to wait for the publication of that book. It may be that it will not be published, for reasons most of you will understand, until I am dead and buried.

I want to talk about other things, though.

I have been greatly supported during my career at the Bar and on the Bench by family and friends, and I am very pleased today that a lot of them are present.

My brother, David, and his wife, Diane, have come up from Tasmania to a place that they think has a principal attribute of being hot, and one can understand why they think that, but it is a bigger sacrifice than usual for them because they have had to come and spend their 51st wedding anniversary in a place that can only be described as hot.

Kay Dillon has also come up from Tasmania, and she is a lifelong friend of mine, and Godmother of two of my daughters.

Geoffrey Barnard is an old friend from Papua New Guinea, and the Godfather of my eldest daughter, and he and his wife, Linda, have come from Sydney.

Brian and Denise Hoath and Marshall and Louise Irwin have come from Brisbane, and my judicial colleagues, Judge Harrison and Judge Morzone, have come from Cairns. Ken Fleming and his wife and two of my good friends from Mackay, Damien Carroll and Darren Sekac, as well as Roger Kahler, who, I think, has come all the way from Brisbane. All people who all shared interesting times with me in Mackay and have also travelled to be present, and I thank them for that.

Finally, I should mention that Eamon and Richard Lindsay are, I think, both here. More than anyone else here today, they were responsible for the fact that I came to Townsville. Eamon and I met in New Guinea in 1970 and his urging was a significant reason for me deciding to come and live in Townsville. Any of you who think that Townsville would have been a better place if I had never come here should take the matter up with them.

There are many other significant members of the profession and the community who I have not mentioned specifically. Can I just say that I am greatly honoured by your presence and I thank all of you for coming.

I am also honoured that this occasion has brought leaders of the legal profession, such as you, Mr Peter Dunning QC, Solicitor-General, Mr Christopher Hughes QC, President of the Bar Association, and Ms Christine Smyth, President of the Queensland Law Society, who have not only travelled here from Brisbane, but have also said things about me which my family and friends would not have believed if they had not heard them from you. I remember that the honourable Peter Lyons QC speaking at an occasion like this said of these occasions that generally, they are much more to do with goodwill than a search for the truth, but my family will be very pleased to know that there has been no departure from strict truth here today.

All of my daughters, and my grandchildren are also here. Their presence makes it a very special event for me. One of my sons-in-law is managing one of the grandchildren. He is here from Port Douglas and I very much appreciate his presence as, when you have a family made up as mine is, any male support is very welcome.

There are other friends of mine who have come along today who tell me that they consistently try to avoid any contact at all with the law and the legal profession as much as possible, so I should not name them but just thank them for downing tools and coming here this morning. I do not know how the wheels of commerce will function in Townsville today without them at the helm of their respective businesses.

In particular, I want to thank Andrew Gricks who has taken time away from his business and come here with his camera to ensure that I will have a lasting record of what takes place today. Andrew has been a good friend to me for more than 30 years. He takes better photographs than anyone I know. He is used to taking photographs of V8 racing cars, so he will find this crowd easy to deal with as they are fairly slow moving by comparison.

Over the recent years, I have had great support from Court staff and from all my Associates. The Court staff do the best to placate me when frustrations of working in this environment threaten to overtake me, and my Associates have worked hard to keep me in touch with what Adria assures me is the real world so that I do not become too distant out in the nice accommodation we have at the back.

I do not mention all of them by name. It does not mean that I do not appreciate everything that was done for me by each and every one of them.

I want to particularly mention the Bailiffs of this Court. They provide an essential service to a Court where jury trials are conducted, and I think they are often underrated or overlooked altogether. Without them, a system of criminal justice in which jury trials are to be conducted would not function very well. One of their number used to keep me well supplied with citrus fruits, as well as reading materials about the AFL and I will very much miss him as I go to retirement.

There is another serving Bailiff of this Court, and I am not sure if she is here today – she would prefer not to be identified probably, so I can only tell you that her initials are Tania Douglas – she did not have to be involved with the Court for very long before she recognised that I was a person somewhat undernourished, so she used to spend her evenings at home making chocolate sweets for me, and recently brought me a delightful apple cake to ease my passage into retirement.

Gary Neilson, who is here today, serves as a Bailiff, but also can fix nearly anything and without him, we would not have a Court that worked as efficiently as it does.

Bailiffs do all of these extra jobs while discharging their regular duties as bailiffs. I am very grateful to all of them.

I have no doubt missed people and for that I apologise. It is not that I do not value your friendship and your assistance and your presence here today, but simply that as I lurch towards judicial incapacity, I find it difficult to take all of this in and mention all of you.

I have only one message, and some of you have touched on it already. You know that I have an interest in advocacy. Teaching advocacy, I try to encourage students to express themselves concisely and accurately and in simple language and avoid hyperbole and unnecessary padding in what they say. I think some could make a case for saying that those of us who occupy positions on the Bench would do well to adopt a similar approach to judgment writing.

Just before Christmas, I read in *The Australian* newspaper that a newly elected Senator had suffered a setback in the Federal Court where his imaginative defences to bankruptcy proceedings brought against him were struck out or otherwise dismissed. The newspaper reported that the judgment covered a total of 184 pages. I thought this was extraordinary, so I went to the AustLII site to check. In fact, it was 183 paragraphs, which is probably not quite so bad. It did cause me, though, to start thinking about brevity again, and you will all be relieved probably to know that this is the only serious thing I am going to say today, but it is a pet subject of mine during most of the time that I have been on the Court.

One can start from an extreme point of view. Many years ago, Lord Mansfield gave this advice to Judges: "consider what you think the justice of the case requires and decide it accordingly, but never give reasons for your judgment will probably be right, but your reasons will almost always be wrong."

When I was newly appointed, I went to a judgment writing school. Participants were encouraged to take a judgment to that school held over a weekend in South Australia so that members of the school and the tutors there could consider the judgment and see whether or not the views in it could be expressed more economically. Being newly appointed, I had only one published judgment to take, and that was a case that you, Mr Hughes, will remember concerning a supermarket at Bushland Beach. You probably remember it well because of what follows, but you would not remember, perhaps, these details.

I gave a judgment originally in that case that consisted of 61 paragraphs expressed over 11 pages. During the course of the judgment writing school, the judgment was revised on two or three occasions and we finished up with a seven-page judgment of 43 paragraphs. The revision was a document which was, in my humble opinion but drawing some support from those who provided tuition at the judgment writing school, a considerable improvement on the original.

The following year, however, the Court of Appeal published a decision on appeal from my original decision. The Court of Appeal, in a 22-page judgment containing 60 paragraphs, concluded that my judgment did not contain a sufficiently fulsome expression of the reasons for reaching the conclusions that I had reached and that therefore the matter would have to be sent back to be dealt with by another Judge of the Planning and Environment Court.

Now, I am not here to be critical of the Court of Appeal. I just say this: imagine how things would have been had that Court seen not the original document but the revised version.

I am not a green activist by any means, but having been brought up in Tasmania, I do have a love of our trees and our forests and when I see page after page of published work of other Judges, I wonder why it is necessary to write at such length about matters which are often resolved by the resolution of one or two questions. Much of the waste often occurs by the quoting of large slabs of writings of others when addressing questions that must be addressed.

The American professor who was amongst the tutors at the judgment writing school I mentioned suggested it is appropriate, perhaps, to approach the resolution of a legal question by naming the relevant cases, perhaps even in a footnote, and then say what you understand them to mean. This, of course, is an approach that has significant risk because if you have not read the right cases, that will be immediately obvious, and if you do not understand them, it will be obvious, but it is a transparent form of thinking and writing which I think exposes the thought process to people rather than hiding it in a morass of unnecessary words.

If we all did that, we would save the forests.

Perhaps we could have a rule that there ought be a limit on how many paragraphs one could write about a case depending on how long it took to hear it.

I have a view that the public want understandable, concisely expressed and promptly delivered reasons, and that is what I have tried to deliver in my time on the Bench.

I acknowledge, however, that the idea does not seem to be catching on. It is difficult to perfect brevity, and I just want to share something with you that I read in the American magazines that I buy to study advocacy things.

I do not think there is a better example of judicial brevity than that provided by Judge David Cain of the Franklin County in Ohio who had to deal with an inmate's lawsuit against the prison and prison officers because he had brought the lawsuit because he had soiled himself after a prison guard had refused his request to go to the toilet.

> Judge David Cain expressed himself this way:
> "the law provideth no relief
> for such unmitigated grief.
> Neither runs nor constipation
> can justify this litigation.
> Whether bowels constrict or flex,
> de minimis non curat lex."

Now, would it not be wonderful to have an opportunity like that, but as well, to have the wit to express oneself so briefly.

But one should not think there has no light at the end of the tunnel because although those who write judgments do not seem to be enamoured of the idea of brevity, I see that it is catching on in Townsville amongst the Solicitors' branch of the profession.

When I was admitted to practise in Tasmania, Solicitors' firms practised under names of the partners, some living and some long dead. So, there were delightfully long names for receptionists to pronounce when answering the telephone.

Names such as Page, Seager, Bethune, Thompson & Doyle, and Simmons, Wolfhagen, Simmons & Walsh were a nightmare for young receptionists whose principal duty was to answer the phone and recite the name of the firm in full to each caller.

But now, Townsville's litigants have a much better opportunity because they can choose from firms with names like:

Emanate Legal - I imagine that might be the sort of place that you would go if you thought your litigation might provide guidance for the future.

Rapid Legal Solutions - the place to go if you wanted everything to be resolved quickly, I imagine.

Resolute Law, a place you might choose if you wanted to be sure that your lawyer would not back away from a fight.

Strategic Lawyers - the place to choose, I imagine, if you thought that the emphasis should be placed on planning every step in your litigation carefully.

Shades of Grey - Lawyers, the place to choose if you thought there were many worries and uncertainties in your proposed litigation.

More recently, Organic Law. I imagine that would be placed to go if your case involved body parts. A litigant involved in such litigation might consider a joint retainer engaging that firm collaboratively with Shades of Grey.

I will not dwell on this further. It is time for me to move on and allow the young tyros of our profession to move resolutely, strategically and, please God, occasionally rapidly towards the resolution of cases of all kinds, but particularly those including body parts in which there are shades of gray, and by doing so they will provide results from which a modern, new approach to the resolution of legal disputes might emanate.

Finally, I just want to say this: history will judge whether or not my career has been appropriately described as successful.

The extent to which it has been both at the Bar and on the Bench, is due to a number of ingredients. One needs to be involved in litigation that is rewarding as well as challenging. One needs to work with good people, and I have been blessed with those things during my life.

I think one also needs a generous slice of good luck, and I have been fortunate enough to get that as well

But, most of all in the busy life that I have led, one needs a good life partner. I was lucky enough to meet one of those in 1971 in New Guinea and to enter into a long-term contract with her in 1972. I have been fortunate to keep her ever since. There may have been occasions when it has been suggested that I was in breach of some implied term of the contract, but at any rate, it was never taken up.

She has been untiring in her efforts to ensure that I am supported both at work and at home and though at times I sense that she regards me as a bit of a nuisance and best kept out of the house.

She has been so good to me over the years that I think she should be rewarded in some tangible way.

To that end, Christine, I hereby irrevocably, unconditionally and absolutely forgive and abandon all and any claims I might have against you arising from or in any way connected with your tendency to bossiness.

The litigators amongst you will notice immediately that that is a forgiveness and release in respect of past claims only.

I thank you all for coming. My apologies to you all for choosing to speak to you about judicial brevity and then taking so long to do it. I hope you will forgive me. I hope I will have an opportunity to speak to you at morning tea. Thank you very much.

THE CHIEF JUDGE: Ladies and gentlemen, can I invite all here present to join the Judges for morning tea at the North Queensland Club, and finally, I direct that these proceedings be recorded.

Would you adjourn the Court, please, Mr Bailiff?

ADJOURNED   [10.49 am]

With Brian Hoath and Eamon Lindsay at the North Queensland Club following my valedictory

POST SCRIPT

I hope that, in reading this book, you'll see the passion and dedication my husband dedicated to his work as a lawyer and Judge. The law was truly his first love, a calling he embraced with unwavering commitment and skill. Beyond his remarkable career, he was a devoted husband and father, whose warmth and kindness touched the lives of everyone around him. His absence is deeply felt, and he is very missed by our family every day. We carry his legacy in our hearts, cherishing the lessons he taught us.

www.ingramcontent.com/pod-product-compliance
Lightning Source LLC
Chambersburg PA
CBHW060557080526
44585CB00013B/594